The Thrill

of

Teaching

Books Available By Dan Clark:

Forgotten Fundamentals—The Answers Are in the Box
Best or Right—Why Great Is Not Good Enough
Chicken Soup for the College Soul
Dan's Most Popular Stories in Chicken Soup for the Soul
Puppies for Sale and Other Inspirational Tales
Puppies for Sale (Illustrated Storybook)
Clark's Children's Classics
Soul Food Volumes I and II (The Collection)
The Funniest Things Happen When You Look for Laughs
The Book of Wisdom, Rhymes, and Wizardry
Rainbows Follow Rain
Lyrical Poetry
The Privilege of the Platform—The Art and Science of Public Speaking
Only the Best on Leadership
Only the Best on Customer Service

Order at his web site: www.danclarkspeak.com

The Thrill of Teaching

by *New York Times* Best Selling Author

Dan Clark

CFI
Springville, Utah

ISBN 13: 978-1-59955-041-1

Published by CFI, an imprint of Cedar Fort, Inc.
2373 W. 700 S., Springville, UT, 84663
Distributed by Cedar Fort, Inc. www.cedarfort.com

Cover design by Nicole Williams
Cover design © 2007 by Lyle Mortimer

Printed in the United States of America

10 9 8 7 6 5 4 3 2 1

Printed on acid-free paper

Table of Contents

100 Coaches

Acknowledgments

For my special teachers who believed in me when others wouldn't: Ms. Dubois, Mrs. Inman, Dr. Morray, Mrs. Smart, Principal Richards, Mr. Croft, Mr. Thorem and Coaches Din Morris, Brooks, Allen, Wageman, Trost, Martin, Weight, Simons, Banker, Zimmer, McBride and Gadd.

For Russ Anderson, Don Pugh, Doug Miller, Fran Peak, Dick Nourse, Zig Ziglar, Jim and Karen Koeninger, Norm Gibbons, Lila Bjorkland, Micky Fisher, Don Wilson, Kay Baker, Pat Mutch, Steve Cosgrove, Les Hewitt, Don Gale, Michael Gale, Chuck Coomradt, Charles Reid, Steve Munn, Wayne and Ruby Clark, Paul Clark, Kelly Clark and Laura Calchera (Supreme Commander) for helping me launch my career and/or take it to the next level.

For my National Speakers Association inspiration: Mark Victor Hansen, Jack Canfield, Gail Larsen, Naomi Rhode, Dave Gordon, Robert Henry, Renee Strom, Keith Harrell, Roger Crawford, Bubba Bechtol, Grady Jim Robinson, Jim Tunney, Jeanne Robertson, Bob Murphy, Patricia Fripp, Ray Pelletier and Art Berg.

For Bill Kimball, Bob and Paul Mendenhall, Dick Clissold, Bill Gibbs, Jay Jensen, Bob Raybould, Lincoln Hanks, President Royden and Sister Derrick, Phillip Gibson, Mark Tuttle, Gary Mangum, Scott Buie, Mark Monsen, Mont Beardall, Blain Hope, Todd Petersen, Colin and Theresa Dunne, Brendan and Evelyn Gibney and Brent Bowen for your spirituality, commitment to obedience, faith and influence in my Christian walk with God.

For K.C., Danny, Nikola, McCall and Alexandrea for finding wisdom, comfort, laughter and solace in my speeches, stories, anecdotes and words. I love you and need you in my life forever.

Foreword

Authoring a book implies that you are a teacher. Education is next in importance to freedom and justice; without education, neither freedom nor justice can be permanently maintained. Parents and coaches are teachers. So are bosses, co-workers, neighbors, and friends.

The mediocre teacher simply tells. The good teacher explains. The superior teacher demonstrates. The great teacher challenges. The unforgettable teacher inspires. The master teacher does all five. If teachers are wise, they do not invite you into their minds and the houses of their wisdom, but rather lead you to the threshold of your own.

When students come to teachers from a strong, healthy, functioning family, our jobs are easier. When they do not come to us from such circumstances, our jobs are more important.

Time is also a great teacher, but, unfortunately, it kills all its pupils. We don't have time to learn the thousands of things we could learn in a lifetime. We can do anything, but we can't do everything. That's why we need teachers to explain, demonstrate, challenge, inspire, and get us focused to do the right things now, while we are alive and have the energy and the chance to make a difference. Nothing worthwhile comes easily. Half effort does not produce half results—it produces no results.

For these reasons, I have written this book. They say that "to teach is to learn twice," and I already have. So let me simply pay tribute to you, the reader, and offer this work as a reminder of how important educators are. Junior high or high school teachers are deputized by the rest of us to explain teenagers' worlds to them—especially, how to succeed in them.

A coaching teacher is one who teaches correct principles, inspiring athletes to govern themselves—it's what athletes do when the coach is not around that makes them champions. A parental teacher is a legal guardian empowered with the responsibility to teach their children about their world so they can recognize it when they are on their own. This preparation is essential to every person's success in life.

The most memorable teachers are not the easy graders who required less work, gave easy assignments, and proudly sought friendship over respect. Ask your fellow alumni, and my guess is that nobody will even remember these "popular" teachers' names. However, the hard masters, even those who were said to be too tough, too unreasonable, and were loathed by the students, are often remembered not with resentment but with sincere appreciation. It is to these conscientious, caring, hard master teachers that I dedicate this book.

Educators

Teaching is the profession that makes all other professions possible. No one in the world would even have a job without educators. They are the smartest people in the world and could work for any major corporation, yet they decide to teach. Educators have dreams for sale; they make more than a living—they make a difference. Young people make up 26 percent of our population but constitute 100 percent of our future. Thank you, teachers. We love you, we honor you, we need you!

True Nobility

A king sent word into the village that he was in search of a new court counselor and confidant. The first subject approached the king, and the king inquired what he had done to make him worthy of the job. The man knelt and rattled off his resume. He had been the architect and mathematician who had designed the castle and the bridge. He had used logic and careful planning to do his work, and he claimed he could counsel the king on how and why people behaved as they did.

The second subject approached, and the king inquired of his qualifications. The man knelt and explained that he was the one who had built the castle and the bridge. He could counsel the king and his people on the necessity a firm foundation and strong pillars to support them in everything they did.

The third subject approached, and the king asked what he had done to qualify for his court. The subject knelt and bragged about his legal and medical degrees. He said he could counsel the king on what was broken and how to fix it.

Distraught and disgusted by the egocentric attitudes of the subjects, the king reluctantly invited in the final subject. When he saw the old, white-haired woman enter the room, he lost his patience and sarcastically inquired what she could possibly do for him. Quietly, she answered, "I was their teacher." In response to this the king rose, stepped down from his throne, and humbly knelt at her feet to pay tribute to the noblest profession of all.

An Educational System

In my sophomore year of high school I met the anthropology teacher, Mr. Croft. I was a tall, gangly, insecure kid who went to class only enough to stay eligible for athletic competition. I didn't know anything about anthropology, except that "we came from the goo, went through the zoo, and now we're you, whoop-dee-doo," so I had never signed up for Mr. Croft's class. But that it didn't stop him from positively impacting my life.

Mr. Croft was a teacher twenty-four hours a day—in the grocery store on Saturday, in the park on Sunday afternoon, after school, before school, and in and out of his classroom. Mr. Croft inspired and taught every student at East High, including me. He deeply touched and encouraged me to become all I could possibly be.

How could I possibly repay Mr. Croft?

A few years after I graduated from high school, I had an opportunity to coach Pop Warner football for thirteen-year-olds who had never played before. To get a feel for the boys' abilities, I lined them up into two rows and had each of them run out for a pass. I wanted to see who could run, catch, and throw so I could formulate a team in my mind.

Two days into practice, a tall, gangly, insecure kid wearing new clothes showed up on the field. I asked him if he wanted to go home and change his clothes, and he boldly replied, "I've already missed two days of practice, and I don't want to miss any more. I came to play ball!"

He got in line, and when his turn came, I threw him a pass. The ball hit him square in the head. He picked up the ball and ran it back to me. He slapped it into my chest and ran to the other line. The time came for his second pass, and I hit him in the head again. With his nose bleeding and his lip swelling, he picked up the ball, raced it back to me, and got back in line.

On his third attempt, I lofted a soft, easy pass, but it was over his head. He dove for the ball but came up nowhere near it. By then he was messy, mucky, soaking wet, and covered with grass stains from head to toe. He got up, raced back to me, and slapped the muddy ball to my chest.

I decided I'd better have a chat with him before he killed himself trying. I pulled him out of line and asked, "Why are you here? Does your dad want you to be a football star? Did your friends talk you into it?"

He looked up with his big brown eyes and said, "Coach, I'm here because I want to play football. And I promise that if you'll help me, I can do it!"

"What's your name?" I asked.

He shyly answered, "Tommy Croft."

Shocked, I asked if his dad taught anthropology at East High School. Surprised, he replied, "I think so."

"Get back in line," I told him. Here, at last, was my chance to be a Mr. Croft to a Croft! Here was my chance to give something back—the first chance in my life to understand the meaning of the term "educational system." What goes around really does come around!

Kids Say the Darndest Things

A teacher told her class that it was physically impossible for a whale to swallow a human because even though it was a very large mammal, its throat was very small. A young student stated that Jonah was swallowed by a whale. Irritated, the teacher reiterated that a whale could not swallow a human; it was physically impossible.

The student said, "When I get to heaven I will ask Jonah."

The teacher asked, "What if Jonah went to hell?"

The student replied, "Then you ask him."

Milking the Message out of Every Moment

Mr. Richards, our high school principal, couldn't believe his eyes. One night as he chaperoned a dance, he pulled me aside and asked, "When did they start doing this dance thing with the girl cuddled up against the guy, doing all the pelvic gyration junk?"

I smiled and answered, "It's been around for a while. They call it the 'lambada.' "

Mr. Richards replied, "We used to neuter dogs for doing that to our legs!" His statement not only made us laugh, but it helped us see the value in raising our own expectations of dancing from the movements of an animal in uncontrollable heat to ones of a respectful, classy, disciplined human being.

That same year, we had an inter-school boxing tournament to raise money for charity. I volunteered to fight and needed a trainer and manager for my corner. I asked a favorite teacher, Coach Ted Weight, to assist me. After round one was finally over, I staggered back to my corner, beaten up and dejected. I sat down on the stool, looked up at Coach Weight for some encouragement, and asked, "Did I hit him at all? Am I doing any damage?"

Coach solemnly replied, "No, but keep swinging. Maybe the draft will give him a cold." Coach Weight taught me to always do my best but to keep things in perspective and to always have fun while doing it. After all, it was only a boxing match!

Recently, I was at my friend's home, and his tenth grade son came into the kitchen. The child, with his speech impediment, told his dad,

"I-I-I w-w-wa-want t-t-t-to try out f-f-fo-for the debate team." His dad had always supported him and believed in him, so he told the child he thought he could do it. Later that day, the child came home from school dejected and down. His dad asked him if he made the debate team. The child replied, "N-n-n-no. Th-th-th-they s-s-sa-said I w-w-wa-wasn't tall enough." Obviously, this wonderful, empathetic debate teacher knew that if there is a reason to be negative, we should not focus on things we cannot change. This always keeps the hope alive to improve the things we can change.

Positive Discipline

I was recently visiting with Mr. Croft, a former high school teacher. We were discussing mutual respect and support in the context of positive discipline. I was looking for firsthand experience from the world of education that would apply to parenting, coaching, and the corporate world. The conversation centered on how to motivate, inspire, and empower others—not only to increase performance and productivity, but also to follow rules and show respect.

Mr. Croft asked for my definitions of these virtues.

With regard to mutual respect and support, I said, "The only place from which a person can grow is where he or she is."

For positive discipline, I said, "You cannot increase a person's performance by making him or her feel worse; humiliation immobilizes behavior."

Mr. Croft's eyes lit up with excitement as he shared one of his experiences to illustrate his point.

"I had a student who disrupted everything," he said.

"Did you send him to the principal's office?" I asked.

With an offended look on his face, he said, "I've taught school for more than twenty-five years, and I've never sent a student to the principal." Mr. Croft laughed. "Most of my colleagues think the principal has all the Band-Aids. No way. Teachers are responsible for their classrooms and for the development and education of each kid. You don't just throw them out when they do something wrong. We have to invite them to grow. We must catch them doing something right."

"Mr. Croft," I interrupted, "I've been to schools where a long line of students trails out of the principal's office, down the hall, out the door, and past the 9A bus stop. They're suntanned! And they just stand there with that look of 'Yep, I screwed a goldfish into the pencil sharpener four months ago, and I'm still waiting to see the principal.' If this is education, we're fooling ourselves! So what did you do with your student?" I asked.

"Interesting you should ask," he replied. "I didn't give up on him, and my research uncovered that this James character played in a rock-and-roll band and that he was playing that Friday night in a smoke-filled, honky-tonk, redneck, biker bar out in the bushes somewhere. I talked five teachers into going with me so I wouldn't be stabbed all by myself."

"Then what happened?" I asked expectantly.

"Now picture this," Mr. Croft continued. "Six of us, in argyle sweaters with matching socks, stood at the back of the dance floor surrounded by teenagers who looked like they'd been mugged with a staple gun. The lead singer had a carburetor stuck in his nose. When James spotted us he leaned into the microphone and asked, 'What are you proctologist-looking teachers doing here?' We told him we had heard his band was awesome and wanted to check them out."

Mr. Croft and his colleagues stayed only fifteen minutes. That's all the noise they could take. That was Friday night. On Monday morning, was James a discipline problem in Mr. Croft's class? No way. Was he a problem in Mr. Croft's class the rest of the school year? No way! Was James a discipline problem in other teachers' classrooms for the rest of the school year? Yes! Was it because they couldn't teach? No. It was simply because they didn't care.

Quiet Confidence

A kindergarten teacher was observing her classroom of children while they drew pictures. She came to one little girl who was working diligently and asked what the drawing was. The girl replied, "I'm drawing God."

The teacher paused and said, "But no one knows what God looks like."

Without missing a beat or looking up from her drawing, the little girl replied, "They will in a minute!"

Practical Application

We don't learn to *know,* we learn to *do.*

It doesn't do us any good to know how to read a book unless we are motivated to pick one up and read it. Motivation comes from answering "why" and "what's in it for me" and from understanding how to use what we learn in everyday life.

> He's teaching her arithmetic, he said it was his mission,
> He kissed her once, he kissed her twice, and said,
> "Now that's addition."
> And as he added smack by smack in silent satisfaction,
> She sweetly gave the kisses back and said,
> "Now that's subtraction."
> Then he kissed her, she kissed him, without an explanation,
> Then both together smiled and said,
> "That's multiplication."
> Then Dad appeared upon the scene and made a quick decision,
> He kicked that kid three blocks away and said,
> "That's long division!"

Caring Communication

To be an effective educator, parent, and coach, and to fully experience the thrill of teaching, we must perfect the art of effective communication. Communication is more than just two people talking. It is more than verbal. Everyone needs HARR: we all need to be Heard, Acknowledged, Respected, and Remembered. The only way to satisfy these communication needs is by being present in the conversation, establishing eye contact, smiling, using the other person's name, genuinely caring by knowing something personal about his or her life, and listening first to understand, then to respond.

For as long as I can remember, our society has always referred to the differences in parents and children as a generation gap. It is actually a communication gap. According to the Search Institute of Minneapolis, Minnesota, which specializes in healthy communities, there are forty developmental assets that are absolutely necessary in creating healthy, high-self-esteemed, caring, and responsible young people. Number one on the list is positive communication. According to hard-line research, young people need to receive support and engage in positive, meaningful, caring conversation with six non-parent adults every week.

When these six adults communicate with young people, they convey influence and direction in eight areas of the young person's life: support, empowerment, boundaries and expectations, constructive use of time, commitment to learning, positive values, social competencies, and positive identity. The Search Institute reports that the average person under the age of eighteen possesses a mere eighteen of the forty developmental assets.

They have less than half of the necessary assets because they can't communicate in the right way about the right things. Adults think they are more involved in young peoples' lives than they really are.

A classic example took place at a middle school in Georgetown, Texas. The principal called a faculty meeting for the end of the day. Before the mandatory gathering was underway, the principal made a large banner displaying the names of every seventh and eighth grade student and hung it up on the wall of the gymnasium. He then passed out little stars and instructed each of the one hundred adult educators to put a gold star by the name of each of the students who they had any kind of relationship with. A quarter of the students received most of the stars. Another quarter had two or three stars next to their names. Half of the student body had no stars at all. What a social disgrace and a communication disaster! Young people represent 26 percent of America's population, yet they represent 100 percent of our future! And this story is typical everywhere in the world. Every one of us, both young and old, needs to connect more deeply with one another. This can only be accomplished through emotional, heart-to-heart, soul-to-soul, crystal-clear, concise communication. Remember, the only place from which a person can grow and develop is where he or she is. We must go where people are, physically *and* emotionally. Only then can we gently invite them to listen, learn, and grow.

Perspective

Unexpected things happen when we take communication for granted. A mother was talking on the phone in her kitchen when her three-year-old son wandered out the front door of her home and down to a busy intersection. As he stood at the curb, his mother suddenly saw him and raced out to save him. Picking him up she scolded, "How many times do I have to tell you? Don't go by the curb!"

Crying, the child replied, "Mommy, what's a curb?"

People behave based on their understanding of circumstances. It sounds easy until you realize that the first five hundred words in the dictionary have seventeen thousand different meanings. Words vary further in terms of the perspective and interpretation of people involved in communication.

For example, when we listen to the ten o'clock evening news, we understand what we are hearing, but we don't remember the facts and figures. We remember the interpretation of the facts and figures. We react based on how the information relates to our attitude, perspective, and situation. Twelve different people attending a lecture will provide twelve different interpretations of the same lecture, all based on where each individual is coming from, their emotional state, and what they feel is important to them at the time. I witnessed this during a corporate management meeting, where a member of each division in the company was asked to give a one-minute description of the organization. They all explained the company by relating what they did for the company. Specialists from research and development, operations and engineering, finance, sales and marketing, and labor all had different perspectives on the company.

For the sake of discussion, how do you think each of these five department heads would react to a company invitation to go to, let's say, Boulder, Colorado? In concert with their individual interpretations, the research and development person would ask, "Why?" The operations and engineering person would pull out a map, rent a bus, arrange for accommodations, and ask, "How?" The finance person would figure the gas mileage, exact costs to get and stay there, and ask, "How much?" The sales and marketing person would share the vision and dream of the company and would only ask, "Which direction is it?" and would immediately leave to go there. Some of the laborers would question if the trip was really necessary or if it recklessly squandered money that could be put into a profit-sharing plan.

This is true, not only in managing a business, but also in being a great teacher and parent. When communicating, it is important to have mutual understanding and to be empathetic of the people's interpretations, sensitive to their needs, responsive to their hot-button issues, and committed to determining what—not who—is right. We must be aware of unintended consequences. We must see the whole picture from both sides of the issue and be prepared for all of the possible outcomes.

From Slums to Judge

Joseph Serrentino, a juvenile court judge from Los Angeles, proves that life is a story.

He was born and raised in Brooklyn. He was the second eldest in a family of seven children and grew up among street gangs and hoodlums. By the time he was twenty years old, Joe had served time in reform school, jail, the brig, and even a padded cell for incorrigibles. He had flunked out of school four times, went through nearly thirty jobs, and was literally kicked out of the Marine Corps.

As a high school dropout with no skills and no money, he tried his hand at professional boxing. He soon quit that, as well.

One day, as he was passing Brooklyn's Erasmus Hall High School, Joe saw a sign that invited passersby to enroll in night school. Suddenly, his inadequacies hit him like a ton of bricks, and he realized that his only chance for a better life was through education.

Joe enrolled and found that he loved to learn. He graduated with the highest grade point average in the history of Erasmus Hall's night school. He then decided to attend the University of California at Santa Barbara, where he became president of the student body and graduated Magna Cum Laude. After graduation, he began reviewing his life with all of its defeats and decided there was one more thing he should do before he tackled the real world. He re-enlisted in the Marines to remove that embarrassing blemish from his record. After an honorable discharge, he entered Harvard Law School and graduated as class Valedictorian in 1967.

His valedictory address touched everyone present; he recounted his life story and concluded with these words: "Do not look for tragedy or trauma to explain the change in me; it came mainly from inner resolution. Life is a story, and, as the author of my own never-before-written story, I had the right and the chance to write it and rewrite it so that it would play out in whatever way I desired."

Feel

Sometimes the most important factor in a situation is not IQ but EQ—our Emotional Quotient, or our feelings. Being a high-performance person comes not from our Intelligence Quotient but from our Emotional Quotient. IQ gets you the job, but EQ gets you the promotion.

Wouldn't it be a tragedy if we let technology completely overrun our human connections? Wouldn't it be a shame if technology replaced the human touch in a doctor's office, and you got only voice mail?

"If your pain is below the waist, press one."

Will they put the Catholic Church confessions on voicemail? "Call 1-800-FESS UP. If you're into bigamy, press two; if you're worshiping the devil, press 666." Let's hope not!

One of the most magnificent flying machines ever engineered and built is the United States Armed Forces F–18 fighter jet. This state-of-the-art weapon has every conceivable computer chip crammed somewhere into its cockpit. It flies faster than the speed of sound and costs $30 million to produce.

To fly the jet with pure precision at supersonic speeds, a highly trained pilot climbs into the cockpit, surrounded by wall-to-wall gadgets, dials, and gauges, and straddles a control stick. To steer the airplane, the pilot need only move the control stick one inch in any one of the forward, backward, right, or left positions, changing the entire direction of the aircraft by forty-five degrees. When asked what the secret is to flying these high-tech planes, pilots simply answer, "By feel. Once you're airborne, it's all about feel."

Feeling—not just flying—is important.

Pay Attention

Jason came from a good family with two loving parents, two brothers, and a sister. They were all successful academically and socially. They lived in a posh neighborhood. Jason had everything a boy could desire. Yet he was always into some kind of mischief. He wasn't a bad kid who caused trouble, but he always wound up in the thick of bad things.

In first grade, Jason was assigned to special education, and the teachers tried to keep him out of the regular classes. In middle school, he was the "misfit troublemaker." In high school, Jason was tagged with having attention deficit disorder (ADD), even though he was never officially tested. More often than not, his teachers kicked him out of class. On his first report card, he was given all Ds and one C.

One Sunday the family was enjoying brunch at the country club when a teacher stopped by and said, "Jason is doing so well these days. We're pleased and delighted."

"You must be mixing us up with another family," said the father. "Our Jason is worthless. He is always in trouble. We are so embarrassed and just can't figure out why he acts out."

As the teacher walked away, the mother remarked, "You know, honey, come to think of it, Jason hasn't been in trouble for a month. He's even been going to school early and staying late. I wonder what's up?"

The second nine-week grading period came to a close, and, as usual, Jason's mom and dad expected low grades and unsatisfactory marks in behavior. Instead, Jason achieved four As and three Bs, with honors in citizenship. His parents were baffled.

"Who did you sit by to get these grades?" the dad asked sarcastically.

"I did it all myself," Jason humbly answered.

Perplexed and still not satisfied, the parents took Jason back to school to meet with the principal. He assured them that Jason was doing very well.

"We have a new guidance counselor and she seems to have touched your son in a special way," he said. "His self-esteem is much better and he's doing great this term. I think you should meet her."

When the trio approached, the woman had her head down. It took a moment for her to notice she had visitors. When she did, she leaped to her feet and began gesturing with her hands.

"What's this?" asked Jason's father indignantly. "Sign language? Why, she can't even hear."

"That's why she's so great," said Jason, jumping in between them. "She does more than hear, Dad. She listens!"

Everything I Needed to Learn in College I Learned Outside of Class

My first college roommate was a big, strong, soft-spoken cowboy. He had a huge smile, was always polite, and did not speak much. When we first met, I asked, "What's your name?"

He said, "Blain."

Five minutes of silence later I asked, "Where are you from?"

He said, "Idaho."

Five minutes of silence later I asked, "Do you live in the city or the country?"

He said, "Country."

Five minutes of silence later I asked, "What is your major?"

He said, "Communications."

Yes, Blain was a man of few words, but when he did speak, his words were always profound. In the first seven days together, Blain taught me everything I needed to know to succeed for the rest of my life.

Day One

We were late checking into our doom room, so we got last pick of the accommodations. We were told the only thing left was an older corner room. I complained all the way down the hall moaning, "I never get a break," until we opened the door and saw a much bigger, oak trimmed suite.

Blain quietly said, "Never say never. Early bird gets the worm, but the second mouse gets the cheese."

Day Two

I had an old car with squeaky brakes. I needed a mechanic, so I asked Blain if he knew anything about cars. He jacked up my car and took off a wheel. He quickly checked it and put it back on. He then opened the hood and fiddled around for a minute. Dumbfounded, I asked him what he was doing. He simply replied, "You've got to do whatever you can do. I couldn't repair your brakes, so I made your horn louder!"

Day Three

We had the first class of the day together. It was Introduction to Marketing. The professor said, "Take thirty minutes and write an ad. Use as many words as necessary, but keep it to one page." After a while the professor called on three different people to share. They read full page, 750-word essays. The professor then called on Blain. He quietly read, "For Sale: Parachute, only used once, never opened, small stain." The class laughed. He said, "Less is more."

Day Four

The sociology professor ironically didn't seem to care about anything or anyone. He didn't call the roll and only talked for one minute at the beginning of class to tell us to read chapters one and two. Then he sat down, put his feet up on a table and read a magazine for the next thirty minutes. I commented to Blain, "How can he teach us when he is not even involved in the class?"

Blain replied, "He can't. You can't farm from the city."

Day Five

Some of the conservative guys in our dorm had already started to party during the week with their wild roommates. I commented, "John sure is a bad influence on Mike."

Blain replied, "Yep. When you put a hard-to-catch horse in the same field with an easy-to-catch horse, you usually end up with two hard-to-catch horses. When you put a sick child in the same room with a healthy child, most of the time you end up with two sick children. To be great you have to hang out with the disciplined, healthy, great ones!"

Day Six

It was the weekend, and I asked Blain if he wanted to go to a party. We went, and within fifteen minutes the fraternity boys tried to pressure him with the usual, "C'mon. Chill out. Loosen up. Smoke a little dope, drink a few shots, get down tonight." I asked him if he wanted to leave. Blain answered, "No. But they shouldn't try to teach a pig to sing. It's a waste of your time and it annoys the pig!"

Day Seven

I was tired and wanted to sleep in. But Blain was up bright and early. I asked him where he was going all dressed up. He said, "Church."

Sarcastically, I asked, "Why would you go to church? Your parents aren't here to make you."

Blain seriously answered and put me in my place, "It's what the athlete does when the coach is not around that makes him a champion. You should come with me."

I defiantly demanded, "Give me one reason why I should."

Blain pretty much summed up the week and the previous six principles of success he had already shared when he answered, "It's better to build a fence at the edge of the cliff, than to park an ambulance at its base!"

Dreams for Sale

The first day of college, our chemistry professor introduced himself to our class and challenged us to get to know someone we did not know. I stood up to look around when a gentle hand touched my shoulder. I turned around to find a wrinkled, older lady with a giant smile that lit up her entire face like a Christmas tree. She said, "Hi, handsome, my name is Rose. I am eighty-seven years old. Do you want to get lucky?"

I laughed and enthusiastically replied, "You incredible, gorgeous babe, of course I do!" To which she gave me a big, squeezing, mighty hug. "Why are you in college at your young, innocent age?" I asked.

She kidded, "I'm here looking for a rich husband, you know, get married, have a couple of children, then retire and travel." As I laughed hysterically, I begged her to be serious. Her answer was simple but profound. "I always dreamed of having a college degree, so I'm getting one!"

After class we walked to the student union building and shared a chocolate milkshake. It was obvious we were soul mates, and we became instant friends. In fact, every day for the next three months we left class together, walked to the union building, and for at least an hour, I sat in awe listening to this time machine expound her wisdom and experience as she shared her life with me.

Over the course of the school year, Rose became a campus icon and generated attention everywhere she went. She loved to dress up and even occasionally wore mini skirts. Guys would whistle at her and she would always respond by flashing a little leg. In the third week of school she even got a tattoo on her left shoulder. I teased her that I was hurt that it didn't say "Dan." Of course, it was a magnificent rose.

At the end of the semester we had Rose speak at our football banquet, and I'll never forget what she taught us. She was introduced and stepped to the podium. As she began to deliver her prepared speech, she dropped her three-by-five cards on the floor. Frustrated and a bit embarrassed, she leaned into the microphone and simply said, "I'm sorry I'm so jittery. I gave up beer for Lent and this whiskey is killing me! I'll never get my speech back together so let me just tell you what I know." As we laughed, she cleared her throat and began. "We do not stop playing because we are old; we grow old because we stop playing. There are only four secrets to staying young, being happy, and achieving success.

1. Carpe diem with humor. Seize each day with laughter.

2. You've got to have a dream. If you don't have a dream, how are you going to make a dream come true? When you lose your dreams, you die. That's why we have so many people walking around who are dead and they don't even know it!

3. There is a giant difference between growing older and growing up. If you are nineteen years old and lie in bed for one full year, and don't do one productive thing, you will turn twenty years old. If I am eighty-seven years old and stay in bed for a year I will turn eighty-eight. Whoop-de-do! Anybody can grow older. That doesn't take any talent or ability. The idea is to grow up by always finding the opportunity in change.

4. Leave no regrets. The elderly usually don't regret what they did; they regret what they did not do. The only people who fear death are those with regrets."

At the end of the year, Rose finished the college degree she had begun all those years ago. One week after graduation, Rose died peacefully in her sleep. More than two thousand college students attended her funeral in tribute to the wonder woman who taught by example that it's never too late to be all you can possibly be.

Moral of the Story

A teacher gave her fifth grade class an assignment to ask parents to tell them a story with a moral. The next day, the kids shared their stories with the class.

Kathy said, "We have a lot of egg-laying hens. One time we were taking our eggs to market in a basket on the front seat of the pickup when we hit a bump and all the eggs went flying."

"And what's the moral of the story?" asked the teacher.

"Don't put all your eggs in one basket."

Lucy said, "We raise chickens for the meat market. We had a dozen eggs one time, but when they hatched, we only had ten live chicks. The moral to the story is, 'don't count your chickens until they've hatched.'"

The teacher then called on Johnny.

"My daddy told me this story about my Aunt Hazel. She was a flight engineer during Desert Storm, and her plane got hit. She had to bail out over enemy territory, and all she had was a bottle of whisky, a machine gun, and a machete. So she drank the whisky on the way down so the bottle wouldn't break. When she landed right in the middle of one hundred enemy troops, she killed seventy of them with the machine gun until it ran out of bullets! Then she killed twenty of them with the machete 'til the blade broke; then she killed the last ten with her bare hands."

"Good heavens," said the horrified teacher. "What kind of moral did your daddy teach you from that story?"

"Stay away from Aunt Hazel when she's been drinking!"

Ethical Forgiveness

A hard-core disciplinarian stood in front of our business ethics class with a crew cut hair style and piercing eyes. He had been a Marine Corps drill sergeant in the Vietnam War, had a Master's Degree in psychology, and was now a professor. Rumor had it that this macho man tolerated no funny business. He explained as part of the course orientation that he could always tell if someone cheated.

Sarcastically, he illustrated, "One time I called a young man on the carpet. I accused him of cheating. He promised he hadn't. I countered, 'Yes, you did.' Again he insisted he hadn't. 'Yes you did,' I said. 'How did you know?' he finally confessed. I answered him, 'The young lady you were sitting next to wrote on her test paper, *don't know the answer.* You wrote, *me neither*!' "

We all laughed at his story but took it to mean that he would "rip the lips off" anyone who was cheating and flunk them out of school.

The weeks passed uneventfully until the day of the midterm exam. A guy on the third row was caught cheating. Everyone held their breath as the professor asked him to leave and turn in his exam early. Surely he would be kicked out of the university. To our surprise, the young man was back in class the next Monday. One indignant student finally raised his hand to interrupt the lecture.

"Mr. Jacobsen, professor, sir. I think this is totally absurd. Here you are teaching a class on ethics. You catch a student red handed cheating, and you don't suspend him. What kind of a lesson are you teaching us?"

The professor smiled and replied, "Great question, and I'll answer it with a story. Years ago, in the mountains of California, there was a little one-room schoolhouse that no teacher could handle. The school was just for boys and had an enrollment so rough that anyone who tried to teach would resign after only a few short days. A young, inexperienced teacher applied for a position there, and the director of the school warned him about the out-of-control, disrespectful students. Despite the warning, the teacher took the job."

"On the first day of school, the new teacher greeted his students, 'Good morning, boys, I'm here because I care about you.'

"They yelled, 'Yeah, right. You don't even know us,' and they laughed and made fun at the top of their voices.

"The teacher continued, 'Now, I want a good school, but I confess that I do not know how to make the school good unless you help me. Suppose we have a few rules. We support the things we help create, so you tell me your rules, and I'll write them on the chalkboard.'

"One fellow yelled, 'No stealing.'

"Another yelled, 'Be on time.' Finally, ten rules had been written on the chalkboard.

" 'Now,' said the teacher, 'a law is no good unless there is a consequence attached. What shall we do with one who breaks the law?'

"Big John, the toughest of the tough, yelled out, 'Beat him across the back ten times without his coat on.'

" 'That is pretty severe, boys. Are you sure that you are ready to stand by it?' asked the teacher.

"They all yelled, 'Yeah, yeah, beat them to death.'

"The teacher said, 'All right, we will live by them. Class, come to order.'

"Two weeks later, Big John found that his lunch had been stolen. Upon inquiry, the teacher identified the thief—a little, hungry fellow, ten years old. 'We have found the thief, and he must be punished according to your rule—ten stripes across the back. Vincent, come up here,' the teacher ordered.

"The trembling, frail boy approached the teacher slowly, with a big coat fastened up to his neck. The boy pleaded, 'Teacher, you can lick me as hard as you like, but please, don't make me take my coat off.'

" 'Take the coat off,' the teacher reminded. 'You helped make the rules.'

"As the boy began to unbutton, the teacher saw that the boy had no shirt on. The boy removed the jacket and revealed his bony, crippled body.

"*How can I whip this child?* the teacher thought. But he had to hold to the rules if he wanted to keep order in the school. 'Why aren't you wearing a shirt, Vincent?' the teacher asked.

" 'My father died, and my mother is very poor,' he replied. 'I have only one shirt to my name, and my mother is washing it today. My big brother lent me his coat today to keep me warm.'

"The teacher, with rod in hand, hesitated and reluctantly asked Vincent to turn around. Just then, Big John jumped to his feet and interrupted, 'Teacher, if you don't object, I will take Vincent's whipping for him.'

"The teacher considered the request and responded, 'Very well, there is a law that says that one can be a substitute for another.'

"Off came Big John's coat, and after five hard strokes the rod broke. The teacher bowed his head in his hands and thought, *How can I finish this awful task?* Then he heard the class of tough boys sniffling and sobbing. Little Vincent had reached up and caught Big John with both arms around his neck.

" 'John, I'm sorry I stole your lunch, but it had been two days since I had anything to eat. I was hungrier than usual, and I didn't think. John, I will love you until I die for taking my beating for me. I will never steal again. You are my real-life hero!' "

The college professor stopped talking. There wasn't a dry eye in the room. With tears streaming down his cheeks, he said to our class, "My name is Vincent Jacobsen. I was that frail, crippled, hungry lad. We all make mistakes at some point in our lives, and sometimes all we need is just one break to get our lives back on track. This course is about ethics, and if you remember nothing else, remember that forgiveness is a powerful part of ethical behavior. God bless Big John, wherever he is."

Positive Thinking

Regardless of whether you think positively or negatively, the answer to 2+2 is always the same, right? Not according to George.

When George was in college, it was hard to find a job unless you had graduated in the top 5 percent of your class. George studied very hard. One day, he came running into class late because he had been up all night cramming for an exam. He had missed the math professor's directions for the exam. He grabbed the test, sat down at his desk, and started going at the eight problems in front of him. He finished the test with ease and turned it in. The professor pointed out that he hadn't even attempted the two extra-credit problems that were written on the chalkboard. George pleaded for more time, and the professor let him take the test home to finish. He promised he would turn it in the following morning. He stayed up all night and finally finished one problem. He was depressed because he had run out of time but turned in the unfinished test as promised.

The next morning, a knock came at George's door. He answered to find his math professor. "George, you've made mathematics history!" he proclaimed. "You missed my explanation before class that we shouldn't worry if we can't solve all the problems. Some are impossible to solve. Not even Einstein could solve them. I put two of them on the board. George, you solved one of the problems! How did you do it?"

George pondered for a minute and then explained, "If I had heard you explain that the problems were impossible, do you think I would have even tried to solve them? No way. But I attacked the problems with a positive attitude and one solution finally came!"

It's true. You can if you think you can!

Wild Man

Most teachers are loving, considerate, supportive, positive individuals. But, as in any profession, teaching always has a few negative people who spread negative energy and gossip about others.

Years ago, I was invited to speak at a high school convocation in Louisiana. I went to the faculty lounge to relax and get my thoughts together. Two teachers stormed through the door and immediately started griping about a student whom I'll call the Wild Man.

"That long-haired, dope-smoking, frisbee-throwing, skateboard-jumping, flag-burning hippie will never amount to a hill of beans," said one. The other joined in with ridiculous gossip about as accurate as, "My wife's sister's dog's mother-in-law told me through the grapevine that he did this and that."

When I couldn't take the negative comments any longer, I found the auditorium and checked out the sound system. There, I met the very positive, professional principal who explained the plan for the day.

There was a student named Zachary who had been a friend to everyone. He was an energetic kid who supported all the games and dances. He had multiple sclerosis—a disease that affects the nerves and muscles. For years, Zach had been in a manual wheelchair, moving from class to class, from function to function.

A month before I arrived, Zach's condition worsened, and he needed a motorized wheelchair to stay at his school. Without it, he would have to attend a school with special equipment. Zach couldn't afford the new electric wheelchair, so he would have the leave the school. Today was Zach's last day. He was in the counselor's office with his parents filling out the final paperwork.

The loudspeaker announced the assembly and invited Zach and his parents into the auditorium. The students and faculty filled the giant room, and Zach took his usual spot out in the aisle of the fifteenth row. Zach assumed this would be his last day and last event at the school. Before they introduced me as the speaker, the real drama unfolded.

The student body president came on stage for the Pledge of Allegiance. He then shocked everyone when he introduced Wild Man—the kid the teachers had been degrading in the faculty lounge. With green hair, numerous earrings, and two fly-fishing hooks in his eyebrow, Wild Man caused a stir among the teachers.

Without saying a word, Wild Man gave a signal, and four football players approached Zach, lifted him out of the wheelchair, and brought him to center stage. Wild Man gave another signal, and two students from the band presented Zach's parents with flowers and escorted them to the stage.

Wild Man then excused himself and disappeared backstage. Seconds later, he reappeared driving a brand-new, shiny, chrome-plated electric wheelchair with a giant bow in the school colors taped on the side.

Wild Man stopped the chair and stepped out of the way to allow the football players to place Zach in his new chair. They showed him how to operate it and moved aside as Zach took two victory laps around the stage. Two thousand students and faculty members simultaneously leaped to their feet to give Zach a five-minute standing ovation.

They were cheering for Zach because he could remain at their school, but they were also cheering for Wild Man, who had taken the initiative to rally for Zach's new chair. His mohawked, tattooed, punk-rocker friends had caught wind of his special need and had banded together and collected enough money on their own to buy the chair.

We shouldn't judge a book by its cover. When given a chance to feel wanted, important, capable, and needed, even the most deceiving "books" can surprise everyone and teach valuable lessons. Remember, "A broken clock is still right twice a day." Never give up on anyone!

The Hand

Thanksgiving was just around the corner, and a teacher had instructed her students to draw something for which they were thankful. The teacher was especially thankful for her own children, who had grown up and moved away. She missed holding them so much.

As she looked at the students, she thought to herself: *This inner-city neighborhood is so poverty stricken; these poor little children have so very little to be thankful for—poor, half-fed, half-clothed—what would they draw?*

Boyd was a thin, seemingly neglected, extremely shy boy who participated neither in class nor in the games that the other boys played during recess. When the teacher was on playground duty, Boyd would follow her about like a shadow and would often press very close to her for protection. She wondered what a child like Boyd could possibly be thankful for and what he would draw.

When the drawings were completed, she held them up for the class to see.

There was a picture of a doll, one of a box of Wheaties, one of a new baby brother, and one of a bicycle that an older brother had passed down. There was an interesting picture of a dad. The little girl who had drawn it said she was thankful that he still lived with them when most of her friends had no fathers in their lives.

Boyd had drawn a hand, and when she held up his picture, the students responded in many ways.

One child said, "That is the hand of God, for He gives us everything."

Another said, "That represents all of the hands that help us." But Boyd had drawn only one hand. His picture received more comments than any of the others, but Boyd offered no explanation.

When school let out, the teacher leaned close to Boyd, put her hand on his shoulder—as she usually did when she talked with him—and inquired, "Whose hand are you grateful for?"

Looking up into her face, he smiled and simply said, "Yours."

The teacher's eyes filled with tears as she remembered the numerous occasions when he had seemed incomplete and insecure without her. Many times she had instinctively reached down and taken his hand and held it tightly in hers, which somehow immediately comforted him. Boyd didn't have a mother living at home, and he deeply missed that special, reassuring touch that only a mother can give. The teacher never realized it before, but she had given something of her heart and soul to this little boy simply by reaching out her kind, loving, caring hand. That day, she learned the difference between being a life-teacher and a life-toucher, and she developed a new and deeper understanding of a powerful, popular poem. Boyd's drawing was about "The Touch of the Mother's Hand."

Divine Intervention

During my recruiting visit to the prestigious Baylor University, I was both excited and nervous about accepting a football scholarship to attend this private, conservative, Christian institution. I thought it would be exceptionally formal and totally unaccepting of humorous, off-the-wall behavior. At least, until the Dean of the College of Business and my football host invited me to join them as a visitor in one of the classes.

An exam sat on the professor's desk, ready to be administered immediately following the opening prayer. Many classes at Baylor begin with an invocation. Ironically, the professor asked my host, James Divine, a football player who didn't come across as much of a spiritual giant, to say the prayer. I knew he wasn't prepared for the exam because he had been out with me and "the boys" the night before. So, how did he survive the moment and buy extra time to study for another day? Divine prayed for twenty-five minutes until there was not enough class time left for the students to adequately take the exam. When he finally finished blessing everything on campus and thanking God for everything he could possibly imagine, Divine suddenly stopped talking. Hushed silence filled the room for thirty seconds, which seemed like an eternity. Finally, the professor blurted out, "Amen."

James opened his eyes, looked up, and replied, "Thank you, sir. I've been trying to think of that word for the last five minutes." A cheering ovation from his classmates broke the tension, and the professor reluctantly postponed the exam until the next class period two days later. That day, each student in the class became an instant believer in "Divine" intervention!

Something More

In a certain high school, everyone went above and beyond to care for others. Each of the school's three thousand students received a signed birthday card from the faculty. If a student's family member died, a contingent of students brought flowers to the funeral in support. When the Red Cross needed blood donations, the school set up a blood drive. When Ronald McDonald House needed furniture, this school rallied with others to raise $10,000. When students were absent from school, fellow students phoned them to say, "We missed you today. You are needed and important to our school family."

A school is set up for one thing: to teach a specific curriculum package in a spaced, repetitious way so that the students can regurgitate their memorized knowledge several times during the year in a test format to advance to the next level and to eventually get the job they dream about instead of having to settle for a job that is left over. That's it. Period. So where do all the other things come from? From whence cometh "something more?"

The Student Council at this school initiates and sponsors extracurricular activities. School clubs, dances, assemblies, convocations, pep rallies, career fairs, teacher appreciation days, and community volunteer work all come out of the Student Council budget and are led by students and faculty.

Student Council advisors teach not only a regularly scheduled curriculum course, but also a Leadership course, which includes ethics, interpersonal communication, and management. They do "something more." They coordinate all the activities for the calendar year. Then, in the summer, they take students to leadership camps and attend the National Student Council Association Conference. A student council advisor puts in at least forty extra hours per month during the school year and becomes an expert psychiatric counselor, heart nurse, chauffeur, fund-raiser, disc jockey, spirit broker, poster painter, banner hanger, magazine seller, candy dealer, soft-drink negotiator, and confidant. Most importantly, they advocate student growth and development to the faculty, the principal, the school board, and the district. School life revolves around the Student Council advisor because they do "something more."

Not everyone can qualify to become a Student Council advisor. The position requires personality traits driven by the opportunity to make a difference—incredible vision, patience, determination, perseverance, creativity, commitment to students, and empathetic listening.

Some of the greatest advisors have touched my life for the best: Dr. Earl Reumm from Colorado, Mr. Phil from Louisiana, Kay Baker from Texas, Dennis Locke from Missouri, Patty Ireland from Georgia, Ed Bailey from Washington, Michael Hassell and Bob Shogren from Arizona, Maris Aldrich from Montana, Nancy Moen from Oregon, Don Wilson from Canada, Mark Herman and Alden Esping from California, and T.C. Hardesty from Oklahoma.

It has been said that the greatest teacher is experience. If so, then the greatest teachers are those who focus on experiential learning. The Student Council advisor creates and provides planning, problem solving, critical thinking, team building, public speaking, and public service experiences that outlast the classroom and positively affect students forever.

Why do "something more" and put in extra time to maximize the talents of students, build their character traits, and physically and emotionally prepare them for additional leadership responsibilities in the future? So students will go into the world and want to do "something more." Student Council advisers understand Abraham Lincoln's famous words:

> A child is a person who is going to carry on what you have started. He is going to sit where you are sitting and, when you are gone, attend to those things that you think are important. You may adopt all the policies you please, but how they are carried out depends on him. He will assume control of your cities, states, and nations. He is going to move in and take over your churches, schools, universities, and corporations . . . the fate of humanity is in his hands.

The Miracle of Casey

Little Casey was five years old when I met her. She was one of the most beautiful, bubbly, talkative, big-eyed little girls in the entire world. She had been diagnosed with leukemia and was scheduled for a bone marrow transplant at Doernbecher Children's Hospital in Portland, Oregon. After the frightening, tedious procedure, Casey would need to stay in Portland for months of chemotherapy and radiation treatment. Her mother, Pam, wanted to stay by her side the entire time, but she couldn't afford to miss her job as a schoolteacher. She prayed and pleaded for a miracle.

The miracle of precious little Casey started in the hospital with the capable doctors and nurses who treated and cared for her. The miracle extended when Pam was welcomed to stay at the Ronald McDonald House in Portland—at no charge.

The medical bills became insurmountably high. In Pam's greatest moment of despair, her fellow teachers at South Albany High School arranged their schedules to cover her classes. They didn't have to pay a substitute teacher to take over her classes, and while Pam moved to Portland to be by Casey's side, she didn't miss a single paycheck.

Casey brought help, joy, love, and dreams to everyone who had the privilege of knowing her. She had been in remission and was on her way to recovery when her sudden death shocked and saddened all of us. She passed away on Good Friday in 1994, at ten years of age.

We pray for miracles, and God answers our prayers and fulfills our needs through other people. Sometimes we don't get the answers we choose, and we often don't understand the answers we get. But one thing is for sure: If God had come to Casey's mother and said, "Pam, you can have Casey either ten years or not at all; which do you choose?" I guarantee Pam would have said, "Give me sweet Casey for ten years."

In her short life, Casey Weiler brought together a hospital staff and a high school faculty, and brought my own mind, heart, spirit, and soul into focus. Thanks, Casey, for teaching us about unselfish service, unbridled hope, and endurance to the end, and for giving us a clear understanding of what really matters most.

Classroom Management

A teacher asked Johnny, "How many presidents have we had?"

Johnny countered, "What do you think?"

The teacher replied, "I don't think; I know."

Johnny responded, "I don't think I know either."

Success is based not on what happens to us, but on how we react to what happens to us. To manage our situations effectively we must be creative and flexible, and have a sense of humor and concentration on the situation's end result.

Effective classroom management comes from the same mind-set. For example, let's say that you are a teacher. Pressure and stress intimidate you as school officials—the principal, the superintendent, or a special evaluation committee—visit to your classroom to evaluate your teaching methods. Your anxiety continues to mount as you recall such visits in the past. However, with flexibility, a sense of humor, and concentration on results, you can eliminate uncertainty by creatively managing the situation before it occurs. My teaching buddy prepared his students in advance for evaluation visits. He would ask a question, and students who knew the answer were to raise their right hands. Students who did not know the answer were to raise their left hands. This way, all students in the class raised their hands for every question, so the evaluators thought that every student knew the answer to every question. The teacher always called on a student who knew the correct answer, and, he, in turn, always received the highest marks that the evaluation team could give!

This mind-set also applies to managing the classroom learning environment. People learn in many different ways; some are left-brainers, some are right-brainers (and some of my athlete buddies are no-brainers). It is important that teachers set up a classroom success system. This classroom success system must account for the cognitive, quantitative, and auditory learners, in addition to the creative, kinesthetic, and visual learners. Teachers must continually change their methods to accommodate and honor each student's unique learning style. Surprisingly, the simple formula for implementing this change comes from network television. The high-powered marketing minds of New York's Madison Avenue advertising agencies have studied and discovered that most people between the ages of five and sixty-five have an average attention span of seven minutes. They tested this theory and concluded that people need a change every seven minute. We need a break in the action or a change of focus to maximize concentration and learning. That is why networks break their programming into seven-minute segments and sell advertising accordingly. A thirty-minute television show usually has three or four commercial breaks. And the current trend is not to run thirty- to sixty-second spots, but to run the new, quicker, fifteen-second splashes repeated several times. Our recall is at its highest level of performance when we've been given a break, so we remember the commercials much more clearly and for much longer than we remember the content of the actual television program.

In the classroom, teachers don't have to change their personalities, teaching styles, or lesson plans to accommodate different learning styles. They need only organize the lesson plan into seven-minute segments. They can move from lecture, to video, to writing on the board, to participatory discussion, back to lecture, to quizzes, to film strips, to tests, to reports, and so forth. This draws students into the information a few times during every class period. They have a chance to see, hear, and feel the relevance of the material, and the subject becomes interesting and grades improve, even for the mentally irregular athletes who are nineteen years old and refer to the seventh grade as their senior year.

The One Creative Force

A college professor assigned his sociology class to go into the Baltimore slums to get case histories of two hundred young boys. The students were asked to write an evaluation of each boy's future. In every case, the students wrote, "He hasn't got a chance." Twenty-five years later, another sociology professor came across the earlier study. He asked his students to follow up on the project to see what had happened to those boys. With the exception of twenty boys who had moved away or died, the students learned that 176 of the remaining 180 had achieved more than ordinary success as lawyers, doctors, and businessmen.

The professor was astounded and decided to pursue the matter further. Fortunately, all the men still lived in the area, and he was able to ask them how they accounted for their success. In each case, the reply came with feeling, "There was a teacher."

The teacher was still alive, so he sought her out and asked the elderly but alert lady what magic formula she had used to pull these boys out of the slums and into success.

The teacher's eyes sparkled and her lips broke into a gentle smile. "It's really very simple," she said. "I loved those boys."

Hands-On Education

Vocational education is as important as every other subject in our educational curriculum. Vocational education is hands-on, practical-application learning for not only technical skills, but also life skills. Students enroll in vocational education as an elective, so the courses require a special breed of teacher. Can you imagine how teachers' attitudes and behaviors would change if every course were an elective and if student attendance determined paychecks?

Agricultural education is an important vocational education course, and the Future Farmers of America (FFA) is one of the greatest student leadership organizations in the world. They put so much emphasis on personal development and public speaking that it's easy to pick out FFA's exceptional young students in a crowd. I was in a hotel lobby and stopped a young man to ask where the men's room was. He gave me precise directions and ended with a meaningful poem. I said, "You must be an FFA officer." He said, "Yes, sir. How did you know?" It's obvious. They are all so wonderful. Let me share one of the thousands of reasons why.

Jeff was a thirteen-year-old boy entering the eighth grade in a small school in Oklahoma. His father was a drunk and spent more time in jail than out. His mother worked for minimum wage at a local shop. His older brother was doing prison time for arson.

Jeff was a special education student who had been influenced by negative family and friends. He desperately needed some positive encouragement and direction. The agriculture teacher sensed that Jeff was lost and lonely, and invited him to join FFA. In the first week of class, the teacher,

Dale, showed the students many opportunities for growth and development available in FFA. He assigned them to pick one opportunity and write it down as a goal for the year. Jeff came to school the next day with one word on his paper: "pig." He wanted to show a pig. Jeff did not own a pig and had no money to buy one, but he thought it sounded interesting and exciting.

Dale explained to Jeff that the person who sold the most sausage in FFA's annual fund-raiser would win $70—the exact amount needed to purchase a small show pig. Jeff's mother had never seen him so excited. That night Jeff implemented his sales strategy. He opened up the three pages of his little town's phone book and dialed the first listing. That night he phoned every name from A through F and sold 417 sticks of sausage. The next night, he finished the phone book and sold 363 more. Jeff sold more sausage than anyone ever had in the history of the fund-raiser and won the $70 first prize. With the help of his agriculture teacher, Jeff bought the pig.

Dale immediately set high expectations for Jeff's project. First, he established that Jeff could not participate in any of the twelve shows that year if any of his grades ever dropped below a C. Since his early school years, Jeff had earned mostly D grades. Jeff started working harder in school and received As and Bs in all of his classes for the entire school year.

Second, Jeff would have to pay to feed and keep the pig ($25 per month) and earn enough money to pay for hotels, meals, and gas while he traveled from show to show. Jeff found odd jobs at farms and at school to pay his bills.

One day after school, Dale told Jeff he needed to walk and work out his pig for another fifteen minutes and that Dale would come and tell him when to quit. Something sidetracked Dale, and he forgot about Jeff. An hour and a half later, Dale remembered his student. He found Jeff still walking the pig. Six months and twelve shows later, Jeff's dedication paid off. He was paid $311 for his pig at the "premium auction" and later sold it for the market weight value for an additional $173. His $70 pig brought $484.

It's been a few years now since Jeff started his pig project, and he has remained a constant A and B student. He has learned leadership skills, raised other prize-winning animals, participated on livestock judging teams, become a pretty darn good public speaker, and stayed out of trouble. Hands-on vocational education really works in building employable skills, self-esteem, confidence, work ethic, and positive attitude. All other subjects and teachers should take note and put as much practical skills into their curricula as possible.

The Thermodynamics of Hell

The following is an actual bonus question given on a University of Washington chemistry midterm exam. One student's response was so profound that the professor shared it with colleagues.

The question read, "Is Hell exothermic (gives off heat) or endothermic (absorbs heat)?"

Most of the students wrote proofs of their belief using Boyle's Law, (gas cools off when it expands and heats up when it is compressed). One student, however, presented this thorough and amusing argument to win the only A given for the assignment.

> First, we need to know how the mass of Hell is changing in time. So we need to know the rate that souls are moving into Hell and the rate they are leaving. I think that we can safely assume that once a soul gets to Hell, it will not leave. Therefore, no souls are leaving. As for how many souls are entering Hell, let's look at the different religions that exist in the world today. Some of these religions say that if you are not a member of their religion, you will go to Hell.
>
> Since there are more than one of these religions and since people do not belong to more than one religion, we can project that all souls go to Hell. With birth and death rates as they are, we can expect the number of souls in Hell to increase exponentially.
>
> Now, we look at the rate of change of the volume in Hell because Boyle's Law states that in order for the temperature and pressure

in Hell to stay the same, the volume of Hell has to expand proportionately as souls are added. This gives two possibilities:

1. If Hell is expanding at a slower rate than the rate at which souls enter Hell, then the temperature and pressure in Hell will increase until all Hell breaks loose.

2. Of course, if Hell is expanding at a rate faster than the increase of souls in Hell, then the temperature and pressure will drop until Hell freezes over.

So which is it? If we accept the postulate given to me by Ms. Teresa Banyan during my Freshman year, ". . . that it will be a cold day in Hell before I sleep with you," and take into account the fact that I still have not succeeded in having sexual relations with her, then option two cannot be true and, thus, I am sure that Hell is exothermic and will not freeze.

Friendship

There once was a little boy who had a bad temper. His teacher gave him a bag of nails and told him that every time he lost his temper at school he must hammer a nail into the old fence on the vacant lot behind the school. The first day, the boy had driven thirty-seven nails into the fence. Over the next few weeks, as he learned to control his anger, he hammered fewer nails. He discovered that it was easier to hold his temper than to drive those nails into the fence.

Finally, the day came when the boy didn't lose his temper at all. He told his teacher about it, and the teacher suggested that the boy now pull out one nail for each day that he was able to hold his temper. The days passed, and the young boy was finally able to tell his teacher that all the nails were gone.

The teacher took the lad by the hand and led him to the fence. She said, "You have done well, my son, but look at the holes in the fence. The fence will never be the same. When you say things in anger, they leave a scar just like this one. You can put a knife in a man and draw it out. It doesn't matter how many times you say you're sorry, the wound is still there. A verbal wound is as bad as a physical one. Friends are very rare. Most of us are lucky to have one or two good friends in an entire lifetime. They make us smile and encourage us to succeed. They lend an ear, they share words of praise, and they always want to open their hearts to us.

To have a friend you must first be a friend. A best friend brings out the best in you, and you, in them. Let us show our friends how much we care!"

Saved by the Book

One day, when I was a freshman in high school, I saw Kyle, a kid from my class, walking home from school. It looked like he was carrying all of his books. I thought to myself, *Why would anyone bring home all his books on a Friday? He must really be a nerd.* I, myself, had quite a weekend planned—parties, then a football game with my friends Saturday afternoon—so I shrugged my shoulders and went on. As I was walking, I saw several kids run toward him. They knocked his books out of his arms and tripped him into the dirt. I saw his glasses land in the grass about ten feet away from him. He looked up, and I saw a terrible sadness in his eyes.

My heart went out to him, so I jogged over to him, and as he crawled around looking for his glasses, I saw a tear in his eye. I found his glasses and said, "Those guys are jerks. They really should get lives."

He looked at me and said, "Hey thanks!" There was a big smile on his face. It was one of those smiles that showed real gratitude. I helped him pick up his books and asked him where he lived. As it turned out, he lived near me, so I asked him why I had never seen him before. He said he had gone to private school before now. I would never have hung out with a private school kid before. We talked all the way home, and I carried his books. He turned out to be a pretty cool kid. I asked him if he wanted to play football on Saturday with me and my friends. He said yes, and we hung out all weekend. The more I got to know Kyle, the more I liked him. And my friends thought the same of him.

Monday morning came, and there was Kyle with the huge stack of books again. I stopped him and said, "Boy, you are gonna really build some serious muscles with this pile of books everyday!" He just laughed and handed me half the books. Over the next four years, Kyle and I became best friends. When we were seniors and began to think about college, Kyle decided on Georgetown and I was going to Duke. I knew that we would always be friends, that the miles would never be a problem. He was going to be a doctor, and I was going to study business on a football scholarship.

Kyle was valedictorian of our class—I teased him all the time about being a nerd—and he had to prepare a speech for graduation. I was so glad it wasn't me having to get up there and speak. On graduation day, I saw Kyle. He looked great. He was one of those guys that really found himself during high school. He filled out and actually looked good in glasses. He had more dates than I did, and all the girls loved him. Boy, sometimes I was jealous. Today was one of those days. I could see that he was nervous about his speech. So, I smacked him on the back and said, "Hey big guy, you'll be great!" He looked at me with one of those looks—the really grateful ones—and smiled.

"Thanks," he said.

When the time came, he cleared his throat and began his speech. "Graduation is a time to thank those who helped you make it through those tough years. Your parents, your teaches, your siblings, maybe a coach . . . but mostly, your friends. I am here to tell all of you that being a friend to someone is the best gift you can give them. I am going to tell you a story." With disbelief, I sat mesmerized as he told the story of the first day we met.

He had planned to kill himself over the weekend. He talked of how he had cleaned out his locker so his Mom wouldn't have to do it later and was carrying all of his books and the rest of his stuff home. He looked hard at me and gave me a little smile. "Thankfully, I was saved. My friend saved me from doing the unspeakable." I heard the gasp go through the crowd as this handsome, popular boy told us all about his weakest moment. I saw his mom and dad looking at me and smiling that same grateful smile. Not until that moment did I realize its depth. Never underestimate the power of your actions. With one small gesture, you can change a person's life.

Whole Person Learning

We don't learn to know; we learn to do. It doesn't do us any good to know how to read a book if we never pick one up and read it. With all due respect to the extremely intelligent and highly educated, all the information in the world isn't going to make us successful. It's like the man who has three PhDs—one in psychology, one in philosophy, one in sociology: he doesn't have a job, but at least he can explain why!

I'm a huge advocate of getting a college degree. We must be lifelong learners, but let us keep it in perspective and always teach "whole-person" learning. Students need employable skills that are transferable from job to job.

According to research by Dr. John Bishop, chair of Cornell University's Department of Human Resource Studies, most employers are more interested in job applicants' specialty skills than their academic knowledge. When asked what skills they look for when hiring, employers almost always rank occupational skills, work ethic habits, initiative, and reliability over reading and math skills. Bishop's research concludes, "An education that does not encourage skills specialization, leadership training, development of usable 'tools for tomorrow,' and a practical bridge from 'school to work' is a barrier to excellence."

The data clearly states that employer expectations are increasing. In 1982, employers expected skilled workers to simply show up. Today, employers expect employees to perform at higher levels. 1982's message was, "come to work." Today's message is, "come to work and be involved in problem solving, process improvement, peer training, peer hiring, safety ownership, team leadership, customer surveys, multiple skills for different departments, and community charity involvement."

The twenty-first century workforce is all about the vocational education and extracurricular opportunities given to many young people. Educators who prepare their students to compete in a real world that students recognize are important to all of us.

Educators teach us:

Art, that we might put ourselves in other people's situations
and feel what they feels.
Music, that we might not just hear, but listen.
Language, that we might not just speak, but communicate.
History, that we might learn from the successes and failures
of others.
Government, that we might question authority and get
involved.
Science, that we might come to know both seen and
unseen worlds.
Math, that we might always begin logically with the end in
mind.
Vocational education, that we might understand how to take
what we know and apply it to what we want to accomplish.
Physical education, that we might run and not be weary,
walk and not faint.
Nature, that we might respect all living creatures, plants,
and beings, and realize how we are all connected in life.
Self-esteem, that we might love life.

Commitment

There is a suicide epidemic in the world today. It affects everyone from forty-year-olds to young students in our schools. It is happening all over the country: South Shore, New Jersey; Pine Ridge, South Dakota; Orange County, California; Dade County, Florida. In Plano, Texas, several teenagers killed themselves in the same week. In Iowa, one hundred teenagers attempted suicide in thirty days at the same high school. One girl died. The school asked Charlotte Ross, a national consultant on suicide, and me to talk to the kids. We divided the student body into two groups. Charlotte gave the left brain, cognitive, therapy presentation. I gave the right brain, emotional, motivational presentation. We then swapped audiences and repeated our presentations. Finally, we gathered with counselors and health care professionals to interview each of the students who had attempted suicide and survived.

The demographic breakdown of those ninety-nine students was enlightening:

Seventy-three percent were on the honor roll. They said, "Thanks for the recognition, but I still have a giant hole in my heart. Something is missing in my life. Please help me!"

Six students were student body officers elected by classmates. They said, "Thanks for letting us win a popularity contest, but I'm missing something in my life."

Three students were cheerleaders. They said, "Thanks for the attention, but it's shallow and fleeting."

Three students were varsity football players. They said, "We were injured. Our bodies let us down. If we can't be athletes, we are nobody. There is nothing left."

In a corporate setting, the students were the "employees of the month." In the community, they were the "good kids." In school, they were the stars with recognition and constant attention. So why did they want to give up and take their own lives?

Each one told us they lacked "commitment relationships" in their lives. That was the word they used, and it caught my attention. To help us define commitment, let us introduce another word: love. Love is a commitment, not a way of feeling. Romance is not love. Think of it this way: If I love you because you are beautiful, that's romance. But if you are beautiful because I love you, that's real love. It's a value-creating love that inspires us to be the best we can be even when the person we love is away. It makes us honestly say, "I like myself best when I'm with you. I want to see you again."

Because of movies and music we say, "I love her so much. She makes me feel different than I've ever felt before." Hey, so do beans. Feelings, emotions, and hormones are not enough to sustain a relationship.

As important as "I love you" is to our mental health and emotional stability, when it comes to commitment relationships, "I need you" is even more powerful. "I don't love you because I need you—I need you because I love you." Think about it. As you do, let me validate the deep, yet elementary importance of "need."

My friend was getting married. He asked me to write a song and sing it at his wedding. I said that I couldn't. He answered, "I need you." I couldn't say "no" again. I wrote the song. Two days later, he phoned me back to explain that his band had just canceled and that he wanted me to prepare forty to fifty songs to play as dinner entertainment.

I emphatically said, "No way!"

He said, "I need you." I couldn't deny him.

If, as a stranger, I say, "I love you, come on, let's go," you will probably say, "Absolutely not." But if I say, "I need you to help me," you react by saying, "Where's the fire? We can put it out. Let's go."

I practiced and prepared my music. My friend's wedding finally arrived. I sang the song I wrote for the couple, and then one of the forty to fifty I had practiced for the dinner. Before I could sing another song, the band arrived. There had been a miscommunication. I didn't want to sing all night; I wanted to eat and socialize like everybody else, so I helped the band set up their equipment. When I arrived at the wedding reception, I arrived with the attitude that my friend needed me. I would have stayed until four o'clock in the morning if necessary because he needed me. I would have waited tables, mopped the floor, and contributed in any way I could. But the second the band showed up, I was no longer needed. In all truth, they could do without me. Why hang around if I was no longer needed? I didn't. I left the reception and went home.

This is the message coming through loud and clear from adults and young people across America, especially from those we interviewed in Iowa. They all told us they knew they were loved, but that they didn't believe they were needed.

In the corporate arena, when a sales champion or outstanding executive jumps ship to work for the competition, it is usually not about money. It is usually because they no longer feel needed where they are, so they go where they do feel needed. The students in Iowa put on a good outward show that all was well. Most of us buy into thinking outside attention and recognition motivates us. It doesn't, yet we emphasize it in our marriages, personal relationships, business contracts, and athletic endeavors. But we desperately need to be needed. That's what keeps us motivated and hanging around.

The tough reality is that we can't afford to wait for someone else to tell us or show us that we are needed. It might not ever happen. We could go months, or even years, before we experience this crucial validation. So should we give up, quit, and kill ourselves? Definitely not. Private victories must precede public victories. Who are we fooling to think that it is society's responsibility to give our lives meaning, purpose, and excitement? It is our responsibility to do something on a daily basis to prove to ourselves that we are needed. The solution, then, is to participate more and to be involved! We must reach out and establish and nurture commitment relationships based on action and participation, focusing on creating symbiotic, desired results.

In a relationship, "I need you" is not codependency. It means "I am okay, but I would be so much more with you. You complete me." At the beginning of the wedding, I felt as if I was not just good, but I was good for something. I felt that my little weird-shaped puzzle piece really did fit, that I could make a significant contribution. When the band showed up, I lost that understanding. The way we recapture that understanding in any phase of our lives, especially in our personal and professional relationships, is to change our attitude from "what's in it for me?" to "what's in it for others?" The best way for us to prove to ourselves that we are needed is to go out of our way to lift everybody else's performance to a higher level when we are around. We could call it the "Michael Jordan factor." Let's face it: we work harder in relationships, athletics, church, school, communities, and everyday life when we know we make a special difference to others. "I need you" tells people how you feel, expressing that without them, there wouldn't be *everybody*.

Straight Talk

Do unto others as you would have others do unto you. This is a pretty general statement.

A note on my mother's refrigerator door served up a more specific explanation. She called it "The Golden Goodies":

> If you open it, close it.
> If you turn it on, turn it off.
> If you unlock it, lock it up.
> If you break it, admit it.
> If you can't fix it, call someone who can.
> If you borrow it, return it.
> If you value it, take care of it.
> If you make a mess, clean it up.
> If you move it, put it back.
> If it belongs to someone else, get permission to use it.
> If you don't know how to operate it, leave it alone.
> If it's none of your business, don't ask questions.
> If what you have to say will brighten someone's day, say it!
> If what you have to say will hurt somebody, don't say it!
> If something isn't broken, don't try to fix it.
> If you think you know it all, look around and see how little you really know.

I Will Do More

Passionate determination is the feeling you need to get ahead in life. To make it work for you, try learning this:

> I am only one, but I am one.
> I cannot do everything, but I can do something.
> And what I can do, I ought to do.
> And what I ought to do, by the grace of God, I will do.
> I will do more than belong—I will participate.
> I will do more than care—I will help.
> I will do more than believe—I will practice.
> I will do more than be fair—I will be kind.
> I will do more than dream—I will work.
> I will do more than teach—I will inspire.
> I will do more than learn—I will enrich.
> I will do more than give—I will serve.
> I will do more than live—I will grow.
> I will do more than talk—I will act.

Why Should I?

I will do more than be good—I will be good for something. Have you ever volunteered for something? Why did you do it? How did you feel when you finished?

Volunteers arrive early, stay late, go without breaks, work hard, and always smile. Why? They are not paid, yet they give their all. Can you imagine what would happen to our workforce if everybody approached their jobs in the volunteer spirit of "I want to," rather than in the contractual agreement spirit of "I have to"? Contracts bind performance and breed minimum involvement. Volunteerism binds performance, simultaneously breeding maximum productivity.

Imagine what America would be like without volunteers. Consider the organizations that depend on volunteers: churches, youth groups, health care agencies, hospitals, schools, civic organizations, sports leagues, humanitarian associations, and environmental groups—in every community throughout this country. Our quality of life would be infinitely less rewarding if it were not for the volunteers who selflessly offer their time, while receiving no pay and often little or no recognition.

What is the force behind these remarkable efforts and desires to help others? Volunteers find the work extremely satisfying and fulfilling. Volunteering builds self-esteem and develops personal skills. It teaches us how to use our time more productively. More importantly, it teaches us that it isn't always what you have, but more often what you give away that matters most in life. It teaches us to place a greater value on what we contribute to society than on what we accumulate.

Our sense of community is the strongest tradition in the history of American values and it's the volunteers who provide this strength. Through volunteering we make more than just a living with our lives—we make a difference and create ordinary miracles. May each of us volunteer to make and keep America the greatest, freest, bravest, friendliest, cleanest, kindest, most peaceful, most helpful, and most courteous country in the world!

Attention

The occasion was the state high school conference for the Texans' War on Drugs. The setting was a high school gymnasium, crammed with more than two thousand teenagers waiting for the opening general session to begin. A young man strolled up to the stage, stood on one foot with his left elbow resting on the podium, put his right hand on his stomach, and casually began to recite the Pledge of Allegiance. Suddenly, a tall, dark-haired man rose from his chair on the stage. It was apparent that he was the director of the organization presiding over this event. The man walked to the podium and interrupted the young man's recitation.

"My name is General Robinson Risner. I was the highest-ranking prisoner-of-war in the Vietnam War. I spent seven years locked up in solitary confinement. I was tortured beyond belief. I limp because of it. Today I still have a hole in the front of my skull from the Chinese water torture inflicted on me. I willingly and proudly gave up years of my life defending our flag and our country and all the sacred and wonderful principles that they represent. America is the greatest country on the planet, the international leader of human rights and of the free world. And you should show this country and her flag abiding respect. Hundreds of thousands of American soldiers have died for this flag. This young man's actions today are a disgrace to everything we hold dear—especially to the very freedom that allows us to gather here today. Therefore, let's do this again."

General Risner continued, "When we say the Pledge of Allegiance, we stand at attention. We place our right hands over our hearts, we look directly at the flag, and we say the words with conviction and pride.

Please, join me." A respectful silence filled the room. He then recited the Pledge in a way that I had never before heard—in a way that touched my life forever—in a way that taught everyone present the true meaning of patriotism, duty, honor, and country.

It's been a few years since that significant experience, yet every time I see an American flag I vividly remember it. The flag is more than colored cloth. It symbolizes everything for which America stands—every little thing and every single person that has ever contributed to making America great. Flag-burners and disrespectful leaders who flippantly mouth the words of our Pledge should rethink their actions. You can be anti-war, anti-Democrat, anti-Republican, anti-guns, or anti-abortion, but don't ever be anti-American. The flag is not a symbol of any special interest group, political or social faction, racial group, or sexual preference. The flag is the symbol of a free republic and democratic society wherein we can all celebrate our differences and, more importantly, can be free to do so. The flag is what binds us together.

The flag is part of you and me, and it waves so that all the world can see everything we have the opportunity to be. Standing at attention for our flag is key. Show some dignity!

Blurring the Lines

Talk radio is the verbal salt and pepper of lunchtime conversations. It fills the editorial pages with letters to the editors. Certainly, part of this fascination with protest stems from the information explosion. We think we know at least as much about issues as those in positions of authority. In this widely divergent nation, whatever any authority chooses to do, someone will find it objectionable.

And it's usually the passionate critics who write in or call to complain. Supporters are less motivated to express their views. Besides, complainers generate more readers and listeners than backers do.

There's nothing wrong with criticism. It may be healthy to condemn a government policy; it is decidedly unhealthy to condemn the institution of government. It may be appropriate to bring down a president, but it is not appropriate to bring down with him the office of the presidency. It may be worthwhile to denounce a senator, but it is worthless to denounce the United States Senate.

There's a fine line between attacking the individual and attacking the institution. When we blur those lines, we inflict damage upon the institutional structure of the nation.

America was founded on a dream, and now it's up to us to keep that dream viable. Americans have always been courageous, determined, fearless, and bold. Who among us ever wants to say that we no longer possess those qualities?

We look to you, the backers and supporters, the positive movers and shakers, to refute the negative complainers. You must meet the great challenge: to reach beyond the commonplace and not fall short because of lack of creativity or courage. All you need to do this is the desire to do better than ever before; all you need is the faith that you will achieve your goal. All you need is to act—and the time to act is now!

The Pearl

There once was an oyster, whose story I tell,
Who found that some sand had got under his shell.
Just one little grain, but it gave him a pain
For oysters have feelings for all sorts of things.

How did he berate the working of fate
Which had led him to such a deplorable state?
Did he curse the government and cry for an election
And cry that the seas should have given protection?

No. He said to himself, as he lay on the shelf,
Since I cannot remove it, I'll try to improve it.

The years rolled around as years always do
And he came to his ultimate destiny—stew!
And the small grain of sand that had bothered him so
Was a beautiful pearl, all richly aglow.

The tale has a moral, for isn't it grand
What an oyster can do with a morsel of sand?
What couldn't we do if we'd only begin
With all the things that get under our skin?

Parents

"No other success can compensate for failure in the home."

—David O. McKay

"If families aren't forever, then what's forever for?"

—Dan Clark

Support

John McMaster became a superstar basketball player in high school. For each of his three years on the team, he was All-Conference and All-State. In his final season, he was named the Most Valuable Player in the league. John's mother never missed a game. Home or away—regardless of the travel distance or weather conditions—she always bought a season pass and was always in the bleachers cheering her son to victory.

Interestingly, John's mother was totally blind! The mother could not see her son, but he could see her. Support makes a special difference!

Special Man

A little boy wants to be like his dad
So he watches us night and day.
He mimics our moves and weighs our words
He steps in our steps all the way.

He's sculpting a life we're the model for—
He'll follow us happy or sad
And his future depends on example set
'Cause the little boy wants to be just like his dad.

A special man talks by example,
Takes the time to play and hug his lad.
A special man walks by example,
The very best friend a growing boy ever had.
Any male can be a father—
But it takes a special man to be a dad.

He needs a hero to emulate,
He breathes "I believe in you."
Would we have him see everything we see
And have him do what we do?
When we see the reverence that sparkles and shines
In the worshipping eyes of our lad,
Will we be at peace if his dreams come true,
And he grows up to be just like his dad?
Yes, a special man talks by example,

Takes the time to play and hug his lad.
A special man walks by example,
The very best friend a growing boy ever had.
Any male can be a father—
But it takes a special man to be a dad!

I love you, Dad. You're my hero!

Ron

Ron Gibbons was a fifteen-year-old tenth-grade student at Kearns High School in Utah. It was game day, and he was the only sophomore suiting up with the varsity football team. Excitedly, he invited his mother to attend the game. It was her very first football game, and she promised to be there with several of her friends. When the game ended, she was waiting outside the locker room to drive Ron home.

"What did you think of the game, Mom? Did you see our tough defense, the three touchdown passes our team made, and the fumble on the kickoff return that we recovered?" he asked.

His mother replied, "Ron, you were magnificent. You have such presence, and I was so pleased with the pride you took in the way you looked. You pulled up your knee socks eleven times during the game, and I could tell you were sweating in all those bulky pads because you got eight drinks and splashed water on your face twice. I really like how you went out of your way to pat number nineteen, number five, and number ninety on the back every time they came off the field."

"Mom, how do you know all that? And how can you say I was magnificent? I didn't even play in the game."

His mother smiled and hugged him. "Ron, I don't know anything about football. I didn't come here to watch the game. I came here to watch you!"

Be Not Weary

Sally thought she saw life change for the better when a widower from her past returned with a proposal of marriage. Nicely attired, he spoke of a prosperous farm. Sally understood him to mention servants, and that meant that he must be a man of substance. She accepted his offer and crossed the river with him to view her new possessions, only to find a farm surrounded by wild blackberry vines. The house was a floorless, windowless hut. The imaginary servants were two thinly clad, barefoot children. She soon discovered that the man had borrowed the suit and boots to go a'courting. Her first thought was to go back home.

But she looked at the youngest boy, whose gaze met hers, and she decided to stay for the sake of the children, who needed a mother.

Each of us has been in her position, wanting to leave the place we find ourselves in. It's always easier to let somebody else take responsibility for a seemingly hopeless situation.

But never despair. God can make a man only from a boy. Sometimes all the boy needs is a teacher.

Sally Bush didn't know when she looked at the melancholy, ten-year-old face that her new stepson's name was Abraham Lincoln.

Take It Personally

One of the country's greatest educators, Horace Mann, was asked to be the guest speaker at a dedication service for a beautiful new high school building. Standing on the stage of a state-of-the-art auditorium, he concluded by gesturing and saying, "All the sacrifice, hard work, time, and money that went into this magnificent edifice will be worth it if we help but one child."

As Mr. Mann exited the building, a parent confronted him. "Didn't you overstate it a little, that all this would be worth it if we just help one child?" The parent asked.

Horace Mann, in his wisdom, simply replied, "No. What if that child were yours?"

The next time we complain against tax levies and bond issues to improve our school systems, let us take it personally and vote "yes" for education!

Interpretation

Let us review a typical family situation in which the parent discusses a touchy subject of curfew with a teenager. Communication is based on interpretation and understanding of how things look and feel different to each participant, so let us stage this scenario with the parent looking at the teenager with a wall between them. One side of the wall is painted white and the other side is painted blue. The wall represents curfew, and each can see only his or her side and color of the wall.

The father asks his sixteen-year-old daughter, "What color is the wall?"

She answers, "White."

The daughter asks her father the same question, and he answers, "Blue." Who is right? They both are, depending on their individual perspectives and interpretations. The same applies to the discussion about curfew.

The father addresses his daughter, "Your curfew is midnight. What good, clean, pure, powerful, positive thing can teenagers do after midnight that will enhance their lives and help make their dreams come true? I wasn't born yesterday. The sex monster comes out at midnight. Don't argue with me!"

"You are so old fashioned. Don't you remember what it was like to be a teenager back in the dark ages? I can't help it if you were a cheerleader for Ben Hur! Why do you want me home by midnight? My friends get to stay out later!" the daughter replies.

"That's it! Don't talk back to me! See, you don't respect me, so you can't respect yourself, and you'll get into mischief and probably break the law! I brought you into this world, and I can take you out of it. You are grounded! And by the way, I don't approve of some of your friends. You can't hang out with them anymore! If you don't grow up, you will never date until you are thirty years old. Go to your room!" the father says.

"No! I am leaving. I'm divorcing you as my parent. I'm running away from home to live with my friends in a loving commune where we can do whatever we want. Goodbye!" the daughter exclaims.

"Goodbye, my eye! Go to your room!"

"Why should I?"

"Because I said so!"

What happened here? First of all, the father is oblivious to the fundamentals of communication. The conversation quickly deteriorates into an egotistical tug-of-war about who is right. Well . . . who is right? They both are, depending on which side of the wall they are on. The daughter sees and knows the wall is white. The father sees and knows the wall is blue. They are both correct.

The second reason this conversation about curfew got out of hand is because the father is oblivious to the fundamentals of motivation. No one can motivate anyone else. We can only inspire one another to want to motivate ourselves. Motivation, achievement, and accomplishing goals all come from within. It is what children do when their parents are not around that makes or breaks them. To be champion athletes or students, it is what teenagers do when the coach or teacher is not around that makes them champions. Motivation must be example-setting inspiration, which must be turned into empowerment—answering "why." Only when we answer "why" can our teenagers act on their own, be responsible when we are not around, and do the right thing simply because it's the right thing to do.

The third unacceptable thing dear-old-dad does is that he tries to change his daughter's friends. When parents try to choose their children's friends, it forces them to have two sets of friends: those they bring home for the approval of mom and dad and those they really hang out with. No wonder so many parents don't know their children are involved with drugs, go to wild parties, or become members of violent street gangs. These parents force their children to live two separate lives.

Don't misinterpret my message here; parents should and have a right and responsibility to get to know their children's real friends. And the influence of associates is extremely important in establishing or changing behavior. When you put a hard-to-catch horse in the same field with an easy-to-catch horse, you usually end up with two hard-to-catch horses. When you put a sick child in the same room with a healthy child, you usually end up with two sick children. To be great, you have to hang out with the great ones! The challenges and concerns of parents in dealing with their children's friends are not wrong; they are legitimate. It all boils down to effective communication.

Whenever there are challenges between people, we seldom have a generation gap, a management or labor gap, or even a lack-of-respect gap. It is usually a communication gap. In this family scenario, the relationship between father and daughter is being ripped apart all because of a failure to communicate in setting the best and highest expectation for trusting behavior. This argument really isn't about curfew. Curfew is just a boundary similar to an out-of-bounds sideline on a football field. The idea is to stay in bounds, play by the rules, and do the right thing. To keep the referees off our back and to keep our parents, teachers, coaches, and clergy off our backs, we need only abide by the rules and boundaries.

How could this family breakup have been avoided? In any avenue of life, how can we more effectively communicate, set high expectations together, and decide upon a shared vision to establish trusting behavior? The answer is simple: we learn to communicate more effectively by putting less emphasis on *who* is right and more emphasis on *what* is right. Remember, we duplicate that which is emphasized and rewarded.

How is all of this accomplished? The person in authority—in this case, the father—must make the first move to come around to the other person's side of the issue. The authority figure needs to walk a mile in the other person's shoes to see and interpret the world through her glasses. This is the only way to establish trust—the beginning of real communication. Remember, the daughter is absolutely right when she says her wall is white. Then, to complete this process of trust and understanding (reaching out through mutual respect and support), the person in authority needs to open the lines of communication further by inviting the subordinate—child, employee, student, or athlete—to then come over to his side. As we team up from each other's sides of the issue, we create a safe and civil environment for dialogue, respect individuality, accept consequences of behavior, feel responsible for individual destiny, and are empowered to do the right thing based not on who is right—who is older, bigger, stronger, or more powerful—but on what is right.

Let us rewind to the family curfew model and replay it with effective, open, trusting, understanding communication. First, the dad comes around to his sixteen-year-old daughter's side of the wall, removing the issue barrier from between them and placing it in front of both of them. They are no longer going head-to-head, but rather shoulder-to-shoulder, working together to find the best solution. Dad is now on his daughter's side, and he can't believe it but must admit the wall *is* white, just as she said it was. The dad then puts his arms around his daughter, opens his heart and mind, and honestly says, "Daughter, help me see and understand what it is like to be a teenager today from your perspective. Why do you have to stay out so late?"

"Oh, Dad, if I come home at midnight before everybody else, everybody will think I'm mama's little lambie pie."

"But what productive things can teenagers do after midnight that will keep them out of trouble and help make their dreams come true? Bars and clubs are closing and there are more drunk drivers on the road then than at any other time. I love you and just want you to come home safe to me."

"Oh, Dad, don't be silly! Besides, we like to rent videos and make popcorn and hang out. We're safely inside somebody's home."

"Why can't you start the parties earlier?"

"Oh, Dad, we also love to dance at our parties and the guys are so ugly we have to wait until it gets really dark before we start the music and want to dance with any of them!" Suddenly, Dad lightens up.

"No kidding? That was the same problem we had when I was your age!"

Bursting into laughter, the daughter adds, "Are you kidding me? You mean you were actually a teenager once? Are you really starting to understand me? Maybe you're not such an old-fashioned, hard-headed, bad guy after all. Who would have thought you knew so much, and to think you learned it all in just one night!"

The curfew model continues with the psychological reciprocity, "what-goes-around-comes-around." The child now feels respect and support. She puts her arms around her dad, opens her heart and mind, and accepts his invitation to come over to her dad's side of the wall where, she can't believe it, but she now must admit its color is blue. The admission comes when her dad humorously asks her to honestly answer the question,

"If you had you for a child, would you be nervous? Would you want to know who you were with, where you were going, and what reasonable time you would be arriving back home? Now that you have put yourself in my situation, would you have a right and desire to know if there would be alcohol, drugs, gangs, or drunk driving involved in the evening?" Accidents are not supposed to happen, but they do because of poor judgment, negligence, and irresponsible parents who are not there with just enough rules and regulations to help keep their precious children far enough away from the fire that they don't get burned.

I don't know about you, but if I had me for a child, I wouldn't even let me go out! I would have been a nervous wreck. I probably would have grounded myself from the time I was three! Let's face it: our parents know a lot more than we think they know. When I was growing up, my dad told my sister she could not go out with a guy who drove a van. One day, this guy drove up in a van, and my dad saw him and yelled, "Debbie, you can't go out with him; he's driving a van!"

My mother said, "Why? You used to drive a van."

My dad blurted, "That's what I mean. You cannot go out with a guy who drives a van!"

Respectful, open, two-way communication is the key to effective teaching, parenting, and coaching. Any group of people can take turns talking, and any educator, parent, and coach can lecture. But it takes a special human being to understand and engage in verbal and non-verbal, heart-to-heart communication.

Get Involved at School

Parents rarely know the whole story about their children's lives. Many parents don't have the foggiest idea that their teenagers are in violent street gangs or are getting high on drugs, because they do not pay close attention to their children. Parents often see only the pretend side of their children's lives.

So what do we do? Can we truly help our children deal with the negativity and consequences of gangs, drug use, teen pregnancy, dropping out of school, and suicide? Of course we can! All we have to do is get involved in their real lives.

Regardless of whether we want to admit it, control is only an illusion. Sure, we can control our children while they are in our presence, but they are away from us most of the time. It's what they do when we are not around that makes or breaks them. As parents, we need to teach them correct principles and set positive examples of what is good and right, at the same time giving them the freedom to govern themselves.

There are two ways to check up on how they use their freedom. First, we must open our homes in the spirit of unconditional love, so that we may engage in nonjudgmental interaction with all our children's friends. Only then can we witness the true positive and negative influences in their lives. Only then can we counsel our children on their own decisions. For example, we can express if we think the twenty-two piercings of one of our children's friends are a bit much, and we can ask our children if they want to damage their bodies that way.

Second, after we have opened our homes to our children's friends, we must go to our children's schools. Because of the amount of time they spend there, school is the very best place for us to get involved in our children's lives. As we volunteer our time at school, we not only develop a friendship and rapport with our children's friends, but we also grow to appreciate our beloved teachers. I guarantee that after just one day in the classroom you will leave shaking your head, wondering how anyone can be a school teacher without massive doses of medication, psychotherapy, and bodyguards! Middle school teachers could easily be prison wardens when they retire! Yet, some parents viciously complain that teachers only work nine months a year and get paid for twelve, their job is easy, and their workday ends at 2:30 p.m. Obviously, those complainers have not been in a school lately. Many serious issues—threats against teachers' lives, disrespect for authority, serious attempts to hinder accomplishment, crazy concepts such as replacing English with Ebonics as the dominant language, and parents referring to teachers as the bad guys—all contribute to the decline of our schools and cut deeply into the positive attitudes of our educators.

The bottom line of parenting is that good parents who really care about their children will volunteer in the schools. They will help with reading and math, chaperone dances, escort field trips, and stick up for teachers in and out of school. It's actually fun, entertaining, and exciting to volunteer in schools. In the elementary schools, you'll find that the three important basics are not reading, writing, and arithmetic, but rather recess, the tried and tested technique for catching lizards, and show-and-tell. You'll see jewelry boxes transporting hair balls that were coughed up by a pet and hear magnificent reports on such important facts as "more Americans are killed every year by pigs than by sharks."

If you don't like your schools, don't just sit back and complain. Get involved, and make them all that they can and should be. If you don't like what your children are doing or the direction in which they are headed, don't just complain and ground them. Instead, get involved in their lives. Go where they are physically and emotionally. Great parents get involved and stay involved in their children's lives at school.

Fear

In the movie *Rocky III*, Rocky had already lost his title to the vicious character, Clubber Lang. Rocky was scheduled to fight the man again and was truly afraid. But his wife, Adrian, talked him through his fear.

"You've never quit anything before, why quit now?" she asked.

"Because in all the other fights my trainers made me feel I was better than I was," he answered. "It doesn't matter that I have the title. I don't believe in myself anymore. And when you don't believe in yourself, you're through—finished. For the first time in my life I want to quit."

"I'm afraid, too, but there's nothing wrong with being afraid," she said. "The important thing is to overcome your fear or it will bother you the rest of your life. No matter how hard it might be, you've got to fight. I think you can do it, but you have to do it for yourself—for you, alone."

"And if I lose?"

"Then you lose! But at least you lose with no excuses, with no fear. You lose with your head high, knowing you gave it your best effort, there is never any reason to be ashamed." Once Rocky knew that, he pushed himself harder than ever before. He came back to beat the fear inside of him—and beat Clubber Lang, as well. So can you.

We are born with two fears—the fear of loud noises and the fear of falling. We learn the other fears we have: our fear of the dark, of the bogeyman, and of the unknown; our fear of what others may think of us; our fear of taking tests or of speaking in public. Fear is real, and we must either deal with it or hide from it for the rest of our lives. What will you do?

Zig Ziglar defines fear as False Evidence Appearing Real (FEAR). Statistics show that 40 percent of our worries never happen, 30 percent are in the past and cannot be changed, 12 percent are needless, and a mere 8 percent are real. Don't let fear make you an emotional hostage. Face that 8 percent immediately and continually.

Instead of fearing the worst, expect the best. President Franklin D. Roosevelt did. Whether it was because he accepted the presidency during the depth of the Great Depression or because he was wheelchair bound, he emphatically reminded us, "We have nothing to fear but fear itself."

The Importance of Being Needed

A father came home from work, and his little boy wanted to play ball with him. But the father was too busy. The father explained, "I'd love to play, but I have too much work to do. But son, I want you to know that I love you."

The little boy responded, "Daddy, I don't want you to love me. I want you to play ball with me."

Put in his place, the guilty father masked his pain in a childish outburst, "Why don't you grow up?"

The innocent boy shyly answered, "That's what I'm trying to do."

The father immediately softened to his son's profound reply. He picked him up in one arm, and with the bat and ball in the other, they headed to the park. One hour later his sweet little guy had taught him the importance of being needed.

Promises

A young Japanese boy was visiting his grandfather for the weekend. The boy would meet his grandfather at the train station, for the grandfather lived in a village on the other side of the mountain. The boy's parents dropped him off, hugged him and his grandfather good-bye, and drove away.

As the boy and his grandfather waited in line to buy their tickets, the grandfather discovered that he had left his wallet on the previous train and didn't have any money. It was cold and there was a blizzard, so he asked the lady at the ticket window if she would loan him yen valuing $50. The grandfather promised he would pay her back later that night.

The Japanese have deep and abiding respect for their elders, so the lady trusted the old man and loaned him fare.

An hour later, the grandfather and grandson arrived in the village. They walked fifteen minutes through horrible weather and finally entered the cottage. Hungry, tired, and soaking wet, the grandfather went to his drawer and retrieved some money. "Let's go," he said.

His grandson rebutted, "But Grandfather, I'm starving and we're going back to the train station in three days. Why can't you just pay her back then? It will cost you the price of two more round-trip tickets to go now just to pay back two one-way passes."

Putting on a dry overcoat and handing his grandson a wool blanket for comfort, the eighty-year-old man put his arm around his grandson's shoulders and taught him the lesson of the ages. "Son, we must get there tonight before the counter closes and she goes home. This is not about money. This is about honor. I gave her my word, and we must always keep our promises!"

Bird Talk

Have you ever tried to teach a bird to talk? I bought a parakeet and promptly started the process. I looked the bird in the eye and said, "Danny," over and over again. Fifty repetitions a day for two straight months! Three thousand repetitions. Then it finally happened. One morning, as I was leaving the room, the parakeet blurted out, "Danny."

Now it was time to teach him his last name, "Clark." I followed the same process: "Clark, Clark." It only took two hundred repetitions over a week, and the bird finally said, "Clark." The learning process was speeding up!

Then something very interesting happened. I got sick and spent two days in the house coughing and coughing. That weekend I had a party. When I showed off my talking bird, I discovered a great principle about why we think, say. and do the things we do. Positive or negative, we learned it all the same way. I got the bird's attention, and it said, "Danny Clark—Cough!" Yes, the bird coughed.

Now, did I teach the bird to cough? No! The bird was a product of its environment, and so are human beings. What goes into our minds stays and will eventually come out. How did we learn to talk, walk, sing, and dance?

We are not born—we are made. With the right input, we can actually become the "bird" we dream to be!

Input Equals Output

I conducted a leadership experiment with a large group of people in a convention hall. I divided the group down the middle and asked half to close their eyes. The individuals with their eyes open saw an overhead projection of the words "oranges," "apples," and "bananas." I asked the group to remember these three words, and then I removed the projection.

I now had the groups reverse roles so that open eyes were shut and closed eyes were open. For the individuals in the group that now had their eyes open, I displayed an overhead projection of three different words "x-rated," "violence," and "sex." I asked the group to remember these three words, and then I removed the projection.

When everyone's eyes were open, I displayed an overhead projection showing "R_PE." I then asked the member of each group to recall the three words they had seen and fill in the appropriate missing letter. Those who had seen "oranges," "apples," and "bananas" filled in the blank with the letter *i*. There could be no other choice for them but "ripe". Those who had seen "x-rated," "violence," and "sex" filled in the blank with the letter *a*. There could be no other choice for them but "rape."

Think about the far-reaching consequences of this conditioning process. There is a gigantic difference in meaning between "ripe" and "rape"! In the space of sixty seconds, I managed to condition the audience's minds so they thought exactly the way I wanted them to think. This scares me—what goes in really does come out. We are the products of our own thought processes. When we think positively, we act positively and achieve positive outcomes. When we think negatively, we act negatively and achieve negative outcomes. Even the way we visualize others coincides with this input/output formula. We each rise to what is expected of us and become what we think we can become. Sometimes we define what is expected of us, but far too often others define what should be expected of us. Good leaders are aware of this and always strive to input positive information to themselves and others.

Mall Memoirs

When I examined the commonplace experience of going to the local shopping mall, I learned three significant lessons on successful living.

Lesson 1

I had borrowed my neighbor's truck to pick up a large package. On the way to the mall, the truck stalled twice. When I arrived at the mall parking lot, the truck stopped again; this time I could not restart it. Concerned that I had broken my friend's truck, I walked to a repair shop and brought the mechanic back to take a look. He lifted the hood, fiddled around for a few minutes, poured a few drops of fuel into the carburetor, hooked up the jumper cables, and immediately started the engine.

"What's the problem?" I asked.

His reply knocked me over. "You are out of gas."

I laughed and paid him $50 for the road call. I learned that attitude is everything. We can own a brand-new car or truck, but unless we motivate it by putting gas in the tank, it can't take us anywhere.

Lesson 2

A mother with three small children approached the downward escalator. The woman's eight-year-old son inadvertently stepped on the moving step before the rest of the family. Halfway down, he turned around, and his mother realized he had slipped away.

"Come back up here right now!" she yelled.

With wide eyes and a determined look on his face, the little lad began sprinting up the moving escalator. A group of us started cheering, "C'mon Johnny, you can do it!"

The little guy climbed and puffed and climbed some more. But he was going against the tide. One step from the top, he ran out of gas, just like my friend's truck. Too exhausted to continue, he stopped and let the escalator whisk him back to the bottom.

Life is the same way. It's a fast-moving escalator that never stops. If we want to stay competitive and eventually reach the goals we set in our professional and personal lives, we must keep climbing just like Johnny. But unlike that little lad, we can't stop, or we'll end up back at the bottom!

Lesson 3

The third lesson I learned at the mall summarized and combined the other two.

We need motivation—fuel in our tanks—but it must be high-octane product motivation if we expect to get the desired results. What do you fill up with?

It was Saturday morning at the mall. An expensive sedan stopped near the doorway, and a teenage boy got out. His mother yelled from inside the car, "I'll pick you up at 7:30 tonight. Stay out of trouble."

For eight hours, the mall was designated as this teen's baby sitter. His pals arrived shortly after him, and they formed small groups, wandering through the mall, amusing themselves by getting in the way of shoppers, making fun of senior citizens, and knocking over trash cans.

For too many teenagers, cruising the mall is the leisure activity of choice. When these kids do get into trouble, they make excuses and tell the police that no harm has been done. Sadly, the parents of these youngsters usually don't care. Such parents think their own interests are more important than the mall merchants'. Do they understand that we reap only what we sow—input equals output—garbage in equals garbage out?

These troublesome youngsters are the product of irresponsible parents. Would you leave your most valuable possessions wandering for hours unsupervised? Is that the kind of quality time you want your offspring to put in their tanks? What is the input? What is the end result? I guarantee that they will run out of gas and quit before they make it to the top.

Stride to Be Better

I was vacationing in Maui, Hawaii, when Naomi Rhode, a professional speaker, taught me about high expectations. She shared that she and her husband, Jim, had been walking along the beach for several hundred yards when she paused and looked back to see how far they had come. She noticed their footprints in the sand and immediately filled with pride. She pointed them out to her husband and commented, "Wow, think about how many times we have left our footprints in the lives of others."

Suddenly, the ocean interrupted by sweeping in and washing away their footprints, leaving no sign of them ever having been there. Naomi was puzzled—almost hurt—and asked her husband, "How can we leave a more lasting impression on people that will not be washed away with time?"

He wisely replied, "Just walk on higher ground."

No Free Lunch

With freedom comes the responsibility to control our lives. It has been said, "The only thing we are not in charge of is whether or not we are in charge." See if you agree.

How many of you are waiting for your ship to come in? Let me ask, have you done anything about it?

When you were in your mother's womb, things were comfy—if you didn't mind close living quarters and poor lighting. The meals were free, you got to sleep a lot, and all your needs were met.

On nights when things haven't been going my way, I pull up my shirt and stare down at my belly button to remind myself of the good old days, when life was easy.

Many people don't realize that they can't go back to that comfortable place. You can no longer get something for nothing, and we should never be tempted to crawl back into the womb. The umbilical cord was cut for our own good.

So why is it, then, that so many folks spend their whole lives trying to plug it back in? The quicker and earlier we accept the fact that there is no going back—that there's no such thing as a free lunch (unless someone else is picking up the tab)—the faster we can start preparing ourselves to fend for ourselves and get what we want out of life.

If you are sitting around, hoping your ship will come in, and doing nothing to guarantee that it will arrive at the dock, you will be disappointed at the end of your time on earth. "Successful people are just lucky," you say? "I wish I had some luck," you say? Well, my friend, the harder you work, the luckier you will get. It isn't going to happen by chance. And that goes for all of us.

The Key to Strength

Little Jeff was trying unsuccessfully to move a heavy rock. His father stood nearby and finally asked why Jeff wasn't using all his strength. The boy assured his dad that he was.

The father said, "But why aren't you asking me to help?"

Successful leaders use all their strength; that means that they ask for help when they need it. Effective rulers delegate authority and utilize all available resources to increase their power.

The key to leadership is to get others involved—making them know that their efforts are important to the common goal. The more you inspire others to do their part, the better things will turn out for everyone.

The Worth of a Soul

It was Friday, the last day of the last semester of Christy's university experience. She was finally done. She would get her degree!

It started out as a cold, miserable day. Christy had just taken a final exam in statistics and was walking across campus to get into her car, drive to her apartment, and begin her well-deserved and meticulously planned party-packed weekend. Two days of late night cramming, an over-abundance of caffeine in her system, and stress from the fact she had forgotten the obvious answers to three of the easiest questions on the test had left Christy a bona fide, chocolate mess. She was tired, her back hurt, she had recently developed blisters on her foot from her new hiking boots, and, in her mind, had every excuse not to be at school.

As the wind and lashing rain picked up, so did Christy's effort to get home. She started to jog. When she arrived at the last intersection across the street from the student parking lot, Christy met up with a fellow student. She didn't know him and had never spoken with him, but she had seen him several times around campus. "Click, click," the light finally changed, and Christy started to walk. Halfway across the street she heard a sound of desperation. Christy stopped, went back to the man and stooped down in an attempt to hear him more clearly through the whistling storm. He pointed down at his wheelchair's tires and forced out the word, "stuck." He was caught on a small rock. With each effort to free himself, his wheels spun a deeper rut in the mud. It turned out this man had a form of cerebral palsy that affected his speech. His muscles and motor skills were deficient in his legs, and his hands were gnarled and contorted. Somehow, though, he was a self-sufficient university student who managed to get himself around in his manually propelled wheelchair.

Christy unstuck his wheelchair and pushed him over the rocks, through the muck, and over to the other side of the street. He said something else she did not understand but concluded with a distinct "thank you" as they parted ways. Christy went left into the parking lot, and he turned right to continue up the road.

As Christy escaped the horrible weather and slid into her comfortable car, she started the heater and wiped her hair and face with a towel she had on the seat. Out of breath and chilled to the bone, Christy couldn't help but look out her window and notice the man struggling to propel his wheelchair against the fierce wind blowing directly in his face. One push at a time, he inched his way up the hill.

Anyone with a conscience would have helped him, and Christy broke down. She was in a hurry to meet her friends at their favorite watering hole, but she had to follow her heart. Christy turned off the car and reluctantly walked to meet him. As she battled the freezing rain, the only thought that kept her going was the presumed short distance and short time involved. Surely he lived on the next block; she would push him to his apartment, and then run back to her warm car.

When Christy touched his shoulder it startled him into a shocked gasp, but quickly turned into a warm, smiling face with grateful eyes and a struggling outstretched hand of fellowship. "Hel-lo," he slowly greeted. "Ma na-me Jor-dan." Christy answered, "Hi Jordan," and told him she wanted to push him to his home if he would tell her and show her where he lived.

"Oh, Thonk-You. Com. Way." With his tightened, crippled hands, he pointed up the street. Christy pushed and pushed and pushed some more. A mile up the hill, four more curbs, and two mud puddles later, Jordan signaled her to turn left into an apartment garage and stop at the elevator door. "Com, in" he said. Christy, with nose hairs frozen, ears ringing, and a hypothermic posture, couldn't resist the invitation to dry off and thaw out before she started the arctic trek back to her car.

As they entered his apartment, Jordan immediately wheeled into the back bedroom. Christy followed to find Jordan leaning over the bed, talking to a woman. "Ma-Mom," Jordan smiled and proudly confessed. "Ah tak-car of her. She ma he-ro."

As Christy warmed up inside and out, it became easier for her to understand his words and his heart. In total awe and amazement, Christy discovered Jordan had been taking care of his mother since she had a stroke four years ago. Christy also discovered Jordan was a senior in school like her. This was also his last day of school, and he, too, would graduate. She discovered he had read one book per week every week for the last four years and that he spoke five languages. More amazing was the fact he had never missed a day of school.

Every day of college, for the last four years, Jordan had pushed himself over a mile each way, up and down the hill, to and from class. His apartment was the only wheelchair-accessible building close to the campus, which left him no other choice but to live there. His father had passed away, and he was an only child. When his mother took ill three weeks after school had started, he had moved her in with him.

An hour quickly passed, and as Christy got up to leave, Jordan reached out for her hand. With tears in his eyes, Jordan slowly whispered, "Thonk you. In ma whole laff, nev-er, en-ee-bo-dy push ma wheel-chor. Mos pop-ple scared of ma. Ah diff-er-ont, not stu-pid, jus diff-er-ont on out-sod. In-sod ah hav dree-ms jus lak ev-er-ee-bo-dy el-se. In-sod I lov an need to be need-ed. Sem God who ma-ke them, ma-ke me too. Thonk you, thonk you."

Jordan then wheeled over to a table and picked up a Bible. Careful not to tear or drop it, he struggled to open it and find the right page. Finally, he pointed at 1 Samuel 16:7 and said, "reed."

"Look not at his countenance or on the height of his stature. For the Lord seeth not as man seeth. Man looketh on the outward appearance, but the Lord looketh on the heart."

Christy read the passage, and the dim, gloomy day had suddenly changed. She had no more pain from her back ache, fatigue, and blisters—no more excuses. "It's amazing," she thought, "that when you surround yourself with light, it brightens up you and your day." The long walk back to her car seemed short and quick as Christy warmed to the thoughts of Jordan's predicament and his positive, passionate understanding of what life, personal achievement, lasting success, and loving relationships are really all about. Jordan had earned a bachelor's degree in English, but he already had a PhD in life! Of all the lessons Christy learned during her four years of college and in all the hours spent studying the required curriculum, the most powerful, profound lesson she learned, she discovered on her last day of school.

Wreckers

I watched them tearing a building down,
A gang of men in a busy town,
With a ho-heave-ho and a lusty yell,
They swung a beam, and the side wall fell.

I asked the foreman, "Are these men skilled,
And the men you'd hire if you had to build?"
He gave a laugh and said, "No indeed!
Just common labor is all I need.
I can easily wreck in a day or two
What builders have taken a year to do."
I thought to myself as I went my way,
Which of these roles have I tried to play?
Am I a builder who works with care,
Measuring life by the rule and square?
Am I shaping my deeds to a well-made plan,
Patiently doing the best I can?

Or am I a wrecker, who walks the town,
Content with the business of tearing down?

Does It Show on Your Face?

The next time you study yourself in the mirror, don't look at how your face looks; look at what it shows. Is happiness reflected back?

> You don't have to tell how you live each day
> You don't have to say if you work or play.
> A tried, true barometer serves in this place
> However you live, it will show in your face.
> The deceit that you bear in your heart
> Will not stay inside when it first gets a start,
> For sinew and blood are a thin veil of lace
> What you wear in your heart, you wear on your face.
> If your life is unselfish, if for others you live
> For not what you get, but how much you give
> If you live close to God in his infinite grace
> You don't have to tell it; it shows in your face.

If happiness does not show on your face, seek it out. It isn't found by doing what one likes, but by liking what one does. No one has ever injured their eyesight by looking on the bright side of things.

Would You Tell Them?

If you sat down to write a letter that would be opened after you're gone, what would you write? How about:

> Nothing is known positively and completely—keep searching.
> The world is full of things to do over and sort out—practice makes perfect.
> Every government could be better—vote.
> The best picture has not yet been painted—paint it.
> The greatest novel has not yet been written—write it.
> The most inspirational music is yet to come—listen.
> The study of space is in its infancy—imagine.
> Only 2 percent of all knowledge is known—study.
> The greatest sports records have yet to be broken—dream.
> Live each day as if it were your last—do it now.
> The regrets you'll have when you die are not regarding the things you did, but the things you wish you had done—leave no regrets.

I would conclude my letter by confessing that atoms never made much sense to me. The thought of my body being composed of tiny particles spinning in space is too abstract for me to comprehend. What I do understand is that through the makeup of cells, chromosomes, and genes, somehow all those atoms have combined in distinct forms to make every human being completely unique. That means each of us is here for a specific purpose—we each would most definitely be lousy as someone else, yet we are awesome as the person each of us is meant to be. When our time on earth is through, no one else will ever fit the space our jigsaw puzzle-piece selves left behind.

Think about your protons, neutrons, and electrons spinning around in space with the rest of us. Only you have the God-given right and ability to make something of them.

Coaches

"If a man is going to quit, I want him to quit during practice, not during the game. That's why I make practice so hard."

—Coach Paul "Bear" Bryant

Attitude Is Everything

When my son, Spencer, was in the first grade, he had trouble pronouncing his Rs. We thought it was cute, but one day Spencer came home with tears in his eyes. I asked what was wrong, and he softly said, "The kids at school ah making fun of me. They say I can't say my ah's vewee good."

"What should we do about it?" I asked.

"The nuse lady said my attitude is evweething. All I have to do is just pwactice." Everyday before and after school Spencer stood in front of the mirror and worked and worked for two weeks until he could say his Rs perfectly.

In the third grade he entered competitive sports. He was ready for the ordeal, but I wasn't. I thought he still looked newly hatched and terribly vulnerable. "Today I have to stay after school again and practice track," he announced one day. "Why don't you come watch me?"

Of course I went. I watched, and my heart ached because he was trying so hard with such discouraging results. From birth, one leg was three inches shorter than his other and he had great difficulty running. Consequently, he was a high jumper, who with one strong leg flung himself through the air, often landing on the bar. Although he became scratched and battered from his fifteen attempts, he relentlessly pursued his goal.

"Haven't you had enough?" I asked in a feeble attempt to protect him from further failure. With tears in his eyes he softly answered, "The kids make fun of me and say I'm not too good at track, but the coach said I can't quit; it's a league rule."

On the next try, he succeeded in clearing the bar.

At the end of the track season, I thought he had had enough last-place finishes to last a lifetime. To the contrary, he excitedly proposed, "I think I'll try out for the Little League baseball team. Maybe I'm good at baseball." He wasn't. He couldn't run, and he couldn't see the ball. He wore thick coke-bottle glasses. Each evening, he returned exhausted to me but never complained about what he couldn't do. He always wore a smile.

"I missed every fly that came my way," he said one night.

"That's too bad," I sympathized. I put a comforting hand on his shoulder and noticed several bruises on his chest.

"What are these spots?" I asked.

He looked down. "Oh those. That's where the ball hit me."

"My goodness! Shouldn't you duck when you're about to get hit?"

His eyes widened, saddened. "Mom, I wasn't supposed to get hit."

"Why didn't you catch it?" I persisted.

Spencer's countenance changed, and his head dropped. "That's what I was trying to do."

That night I cried myself to sleep wondering if and when he would ever really succeed. The next day I picked him up from practice and he had his new uniform. He ran to the car with the blue and gold jersey slung over his shoulder, and a smile lit up his face like a Christmas tree.

"I got a uniform," he announced. "There were only twelve of them. Most guys did not get one. This was the last uniform, and the coach gave it to me. He said I'd earned it."

"Way to go," I said. It was wonderful to see him so happy.

The bench-warming period began after that, and although he never missed a practice or a game, I lost interest. Rationalizing that I had something better to do than just sit on a hard bleacher and watch my son sit there, I stopped going. Spencer pleaded for me to cancel my Friday evening date and come to his final game. I arrived late but still in time to see him play. I guess Spencer's persistence had finally gotten to the coach and he put him in the game. In the sixth inning, the ball was hit his way. Spencer hobbled as fast as he could but missed it. Three more times he missed it, letting the other team catch up. Then when it was his turn to bat, he struck out. Each mistake was announced over the loud speaker. I was mortified, but somehow Spencer was not. After his poor performance, I thought for sure Spencer would be pulled from the game. The score was close, and they needed a victory to win the championship.

To everyone's surprise, the coach yelled to the end of the bench, "Spencer, you're back in." As Spencer walked past the bleachers he looked up at me and the other parents, and with his patented positiveness he re-assuredly cautioned, "Whoa, mom, we are only ahead by one run, and I don't know if even I can hold them off with only one inning to play!"

We laughed; he was dead serious! No one seemed to worry, though, because this time Spencer was put in right field where no balls had been hit all game long.

There were two quick hits with the winning run now on first base. Then two quick outs. The third hit came Spencer's way. I saw the coach wince and cover his eyes. The ball sailed right into Spencer's glove. We stood to cheer until he collided with another player. He lay motionless. The other player got up and screamed that Spencer's nose was gushing blood. "I think he's dead!" he shouted. "You'd better come quick." With the winning run crossing home plate, the ball park hushed in concerned silence, and the coach jogged his way out of the dugout to administer first aid. Suddenly, Spencer raised his hand in the air. The ball had stayed in his glove. The umpire yelled, "You're out," and our bleachers erupted into a cheering standing ovation. Spencer's team had won the game! The coach stopped walking. He couldn't believe it—no one could. With tears in his eyes, he too, proudly started to clap. Then, in a spontaneous eruption of sportsmanship, the other team started to clap. Although they had just lost the game, one by one the opposing team members stood. Within a minute, the other fans, the two umpires, the other team's coaches, and all of the players on both teams were on their feet cheering for this true eight-year-old hero.

My Spencer is now thirteen years old. It has been five years since that amazing day, and I've never missed another one of his extracurricular activities. In fact, I've stopped procrastinating, changed my previous life perception from half empty to half full, stopped whining about my job layoff, got more education and training (which landed me more fulfilling employment), and never missed another day of work or a day at the gym since then. How could I when I know that attitude is everything!

The Competitive Advantage

If plants grow from sunlight, people grow from praise. So give it freely—it costs nothing and it nourishes. Giving compliments always comes back to you, in one form or another. If you give it, you'll receive it, and everybody likes to hear they've done a job well.

Put this theory to test: start fertilizing your social circle with some recognition and praise. You'll see the difference soon enough.

Everyone needs praise. When we receive it, we grow; without it, we shrink and fade. Look for an occasion to give an encouraging word or a compliment. Strive to make people feel wanted, important, and capable. Let them know they can succeed. Doing this forces us to concentrate on the positive side of people instead of the negative. This makes us all more productive and pleasant to be around.

In sales we call this psychological reciprocity, which simply means that in the course of our conversation, if I make you feel intelligent, significant, special, and important, you subconsciously feel obligated to make me feel equally intelligent, significant, special, and important before the conversation ends.

This psychological reciprocity gives people the competitive advantage. Use it, and you'll see that what goes around comes around!

Support

A high school in northern Utah initiated a unique directive that fully integrated students with physical or mental challenges into the mainstream classes and curriculum. To make it work, the administration organized a mentor program that teamed up every special-needs student with a mainstream student who would help him or her succeed.

The athletic director presented the idea to John, the captain of the football team. John was a tall, strong, intense young man—not the patient, caring type usually needed for this kind of program. He made it clear that this "wasn't his thing," and that he didn't have time to be a mentor. But the athletic director knew it would be good for him and insisted that John volunteer.

John was paired up with Randy, a young man with Down's syndrome. From the minute they were introduced, they were always together. Reluctant and irritated at first, John tried to ditch Randy, but soon John welcomed the constant company. Randy not only attended every one of John's classes and ate with him at lunch, but he also came to John's football practice. After a few days, John asked the coach to make Randy the official team manager, responsible for the balls, tape, and water bottles. At the end of the football season, the team won the state championship, and John was awarded the gold medal as the Most Valuable Player in the state. In gratitude for his services, the team presented Randy with a school letter jacket, and they cheered as Randy put it on. It was the coolest thing that had ever happened to him; from that day forward Randy never took it off. He slept in his jacket and wore it throughout each weekend.

Later that year, John became the captain and star of the basketball team. At John's request, Randy was again named the manager. They were still inseparable throughout the basketball season. Not only did John take Randy to special occasions—like dances, as a joint escort for his girlfriend—but he also took Randy to the library to tutor him in his classes. As he tutored Randy, John became a much better student and made the honor roll for the first time in over a year. The year of the mentor program unveiled itself as the most rewarding year of John's life.

One day tragedy struck in the middle of the state basketball tournament. Randy had caught a virus and suddenly died of pneumonia. The funeral was held the day before the final championship game. John was asked to be one of the speakers. In his eulogy, John shared his deep, abiding friendship and respect for Randy. He told how Randy had been the one who had taught him about real courage, self-esteem, unconditional love, and the importance of effort and perseverance. John dedicated the upcoming state finals game to Randy and concluded his remarks by stating that he was honored to have received the Most Valuable Player award in football and the Leadership Plaque for being the captain of the basketball team. "But," John added, "the real leader of both the football and basketball teams was Randy, for he accomplished more with what he had than anyone I've ever met. Randy inspired all who knew him."

John walked from behind the podium, took off the irreplaceable, twenty-four-carat-gold state football MVP medallion that hung around his neck, leaned into the open casket, and placed it on Randy's chest. He placed his captain's plaque next to it.

Randy was buried in his letter jacket, surrounded by John's cherished awards and pictures and letters left by others who admired him. But this is not the end. The next day John's team won the championship and presented the game ball to Randy's family. John went to college on a full athletic scholarship and graduated with a master's degree in education. Today, John is a special education teacher and volunteers ten hours every week for the Special Olympics.

Needed?

I was speaking to members of Our Primary Purpose (OPP), a highly acclaimed program for chemically dependent teenagers in Des Moines, Iowa. At the third meeting, which was just for parents, a mother shared this story.

Her twenty-year-old son John—who, incidentally, was not enrolled in the OPP program—was handsome and talented, a good citizen, a good student, a good musician, and a good athlete. He also had a lovely girlfriend and seemingly no problems. One day he stopped talking as much as he usually did. Thirty days passed, and his conversation dwindled to nothing. He was depressed, and his parents and girlfriend continually told him that they loved him. He knew that they loved him, and he expressed his love for them. Everyone was concerned about his well-being and wondered what they could say or do to help him, since "I love you" obviously wasn't enough to improve the situation.

John eventually made a move: he locked himself in the cellar. Although he was down in the dim dampness for three days without food, he continued to acknowledge his parents' love for him and his love for them. His depression deepened, and his loved ones were convinced that suicide was imminent. His parents brought in health care professionals, but their love and kind counseling had no effect on John.

On the third day of John's isolation, the local high school football coach—who, incidentally, didn't know what was going on in John's life—called to talk to John. John's mother said that he was busy and took a message at the coach's request. Then she went to the cellar door and called down the stairs, "John, Coach Ivers just phoned. He said that his players voted last night on who they wanted as their assistant coach. They said you were the greatest Pop Warner football coach they had ever had, and now they think they can win the state championship if you help coach them. Coach Ivers said they need you—he needs you! He said if you're interested, you should be at football practice at 2:45 this afternoon."

Do you know what happened? Sure, you do! John came out of the cellar and went to practice. He accepted the coaching job, and by the time he came home from his first practice, he had snapped out of his depression. He once again felt needed, wanted, and important and was back to his old self.

Never Say Never

Richard Nelson, a sixteen-year-old junior at Manti High School in Utah, was an outstanding athlete. He was the number two singles player on the state championship tennis team and had just made the basketball team that would win the state championship later that year. He was looking forward to much success as a senior during the following season. But on October 23, 1966, most of his athletic future was suddenly taken away from him.

Richard was riding his bicycle at night from Manti to Gunnison, where his girlfriend lived. The road was very steep in some places, and Richard reached speeds of forty miles per hour on the downhill slopes. It was dark and he couldn't see well, so Richard followed the white line on the shoulder of the road to ensure his safety. As he came around a blind curve and was looking down at the ground, Richard failed to see a parked car on his side of the road. With no warning, he hit the parked car and was taken to the hospital, where he didn't regain consciousness for another two days. Besides bad cuts on his head and knee, he had broken his collarbone and right arm, necessitating that he wear an L-shaped cast on his arm for two months. The cast came off in late December, and Richard's doctor administered a series of tests to determine the success of his healing. He failed all the tests. His triceps muscle had lost all its strength—he could not push out with his arm. The doctor diagnosed that he had suffered a pinched nerve and that he might never regain the use of his right arm. Richard's once strong but now puny right arm just hung at his side and the doctor gave him no real hope of recovery.

Richard wasn't able to play on the basketball team during the rest of that year, but the coach did make him equipment and statistics manager so that he could come to practice and be around the guys on the team.

His junior year ended, and Richard was determined to do whatever he had to do to make the basketball team the next year. He realized that he couldn't make it right-handed, so he started working on his left-handed skills. Every night, all summer long, he practiced making left-handed baskets at the outdoor tennis courts in the center of town. Every night he shot two hundred left-handed baskets and practiced left-handed dribbling and left-handed passing off the park retaining wall. Instead of going with his friends to the summer dances sponsored by the high school, Richard practiced basketball.

When the next season arrived, Richard was ready to try out for the team—and he made it! He never became a starter, but he was always the first substitute to go in the game.

The season boiled down to the final game of the year against their arch rival, Richfield High. This game would determine which team would win the league championship and advance to the state playoff tournament. It was a "must win" for both teams.

It was Friday night and the gym was packed. The starting guard for Manti had sprained his ankle earlier in the week, so Richard finally got his big break—he started the game! However, before the first quarter was over, Richard was replaced. It was hard to compete when he could only use one arm. The game continued until the last thirty seconds when Manti's other guard was injured, forcing Richard back into the game. Richfield was ahead by three points, and Manti had the ball. The Richfield coach tried to take advantage of the situation by having one of his players immediately foul Richard. Undaunted, Richard stepped up to the free throw line with a one-and-one situation (if he made the first foul shot, he would get a chance to shoot and make a second basket). Confidently, Richard picked up the ball, braced it in his left hand, and shot. Swish! He made it and the crowd went wild! He then made the next shot, bringing Manti High to within one point of Richfield. The crowd stood and went crazy again.

Richfield then took the ball out of bounds and threw a long pass down court to the player Richard was guarding, trying to make a quick, easy basket. But Richard, with his undying determination, leaped through the air to intercept the pass. When he landed he was fouled again, giving him another one-and-one opportunity at the free throw line. With ten seconds left on the clock, Richard balanced the ball in his left hand, took a deep breath, and shot. The crowd was deathly quiet until—swish! He had tied the game! His next shot went up, down, and through! Swish, again! He made it—he made all four shots—left-handed! Richard Nelson won the game and became the hero of the school. And how and why was he able to do it?

According to Richard Nelson, he was not a hero. "Anybody could have done what I did," he said in his post-game interview. "I was supposed to make those shots. Everybody was counting on me to win the game when I was put in that situation. All I did was believe in myself, work hard when others didn't, and persevere. Anybody could have done what I did in the game if they had shot as many foul shots as I had shot last summer in practice. As Earl Nightingale said, 'The only difference between a successful person and an unsuccessful person is that the successful person will do what the unsuccessful person will not do. The key is the successful person does not want to do it either, but then does it anyway.'"

Attitude

It was the third game of Danny's sophomore year. His University of Utah football team had not yet won a game, and they had just been beaten by more than twenty points by a much inferior, last place team. It was the day after the game, and Danny's team was assembled in the meeting room watching the game films of the embarrassing loss. Suddenly, the coach yelled, "Stop the projector. Run that play again."

To the team, the play was not that impressive. The opposing team's running back got the ball and ran around the end with a Utah player coming up and hitting him hard. The Utah player bounced off their guy who continued to run down the field for an additional twenty-five yards before he was finally tackled from behind. This play impressed the Utah coach so much that he rewound and watched the play seven times in a row. He finally said, "Turn off the projector, turn on the lights, and listen to what I'm about to teach you.

"It appears to me that only one player on our team understands the key to winning success. When our guy Danny came up and hit their guy, it was obvious in the film that Danny bounced off and missed the tackle! But Danny was the same guy who tackled their guy twenty-five yards down the field. Danny wasn't even supposed to play or see any action. He was third string on the depth chart. But when the first two players ahead of him got injured, Danny was put in the game. From now on Danny will start every game. He is my kind of guy. You see, Danny's attitude is right. And when your attitude is right, your abilities will always catch up!"

Goals and Why They Exist

Winning is only an excuse to play the game, so we must learn to appreciate the daily practice that prepares us—even when it's a grueling workout. Remember, happiness is not in the destination; it's in the journey. Having said this, let me say a few words about motivation.

I was asked to speak to a group of fathers and sons about setting goals. We were in an auditorium with no basketball standards around, so it was the perfect place to show the guys how important goals are.

One of the boys in the audience had a basketball with him, so I had him come forward with it. I told him to dribble a few times and to shoot a basket. The boy followed my instructions, shaking his head. He shot.

"Did you make it?" I asked.

"No," he said grumpily. "There aren't any baskets. There isn't anything to shoot for!"

With that simple answer, I had made the point I wanted to make. Nobody would want to play basketball without any hoops to shoot for. There would be no point to it, no way to keep score. And everybody wants to know if they have won or lost.

Life is the same way. You need goals if you want to score and feel good about life. Targets show us where we've been and where we still have to go. It's always comforting to see the finish line so we know how far we have to run.

Remember, if you go through life without ambitions, you'll never make the grade. There is only one way to really play the game, whether it's basketball or the game of life.

Aim for something, and shoot to score!

Discipline

Responsibility brings freedom, and freedom provides opportunity. That's the principle of self-discipline.

Self-discipline sounds like some kind of punishment you administer to yourself. It really means you are in control of your actions and of their outcomes—at least to some degree.

Self-discipline means avoiding outside discipline by doing the right thing. Arabian horses are a perfect example of the kind of self-control each of us is capable of achieving. These magnificent horses, with intelligent eyes, well-formed heads, and flowing manes and tails, win many championships because of their stamina and courage.

While they are all hearty specimens, some stand above the others for endurance and intelligence. To identify these exceptional animals, trainers teach them to drink only when they hear a whistle. Once they have learned to obey, they are placed in a corral under the hot sun until they are parched. Trainers place water outside the corral out of the horses' reach, forcing them to wait even longer. Finally, a gate is opened, and most horses stampede for the trough to drink with reckless abandon. Only a few stand poised with pride, holding their heads erect, and don't give in to the terrible craving. Only when they hear the whistle do they allow themselves to drink.

The ones who obey and resist the urge to drink are reserved for special training. The other steeds are led away.

So it is with humans. The mark of a champion is not on the outside, but somewhere deep inside, where self-control resides. To gain control of yourself and become self-disciplined is the second step to becoming successful. First, see yourself as a conqueror. Then, discipline yourself to become one.

Unfortunately, many folks who see themselves as champions are not willing to put in the extra effort and self-discipline to become winners. Consequently, they lose out to those with restraint.

Halftime Score

In our highly competitive world, we must understand that there is nothing more insignificant than the halftime score.

When I was in college at the University of Utah, we played football against UCLA. Before the game, our coach pepped us up, "UCLA doesn't have to win this game. You can win if you think you can. Just believe in yourselves. We can win!"

The game started, and we got the ball first. UCLA quickly took it away from us. It was our turn to stop them. The guy in front of me was so big I had to look through his legs to see what was going on. He could have kick-started a 747 jet! When they hiked the ball, he hit me so hard that he knocked my helmet around my head so that I was looking out my ear hole. As I stood there crying, I realized that my coach had been lying. *UCLA does have to win, and I quit,* I thought to myself as I started to walk off the field. The coach wouldn't let me quit, and he pushed me back into the huddle. The next play, I sacked the quarterback. I have to admit that I ran into him by accident, but I still tackled him for a loss, and he fumbled the ball. We recovered and scored. We stopped them and scored twice more. The halftime score was 19–0, in favor of the University of Utah. During the first half, UCLA's quarterback thought he had been caught in one of those revolving doors at the mall, but we eventually lost the game, 23–19.

On another occasion we played the University of Oklahoma. We were ahead, 7–0. Yes, we were whipping 'em. It was those last fifty-nine minutes that killed us! We lost, 63–7.

In another game, against the University of Arizona, we were behind at halftime, 21–0. However, this time we won, during the last seconds of the game, 28–27!

We also beat Jim McMahon's BYU team. We were losing at halftime but came from behind to win, on a last-second pass, by 23–22.

What is the point? Teams that are ahead at halftime are faced with a decision. They either keep fighting and playing to win or stop taking risks, try to live off their past successes, and start playing "not to lose." Playing "not to lose" is when we stop our aggressive offense and replace it with defensive carefulness. It's when we lose that eye-of-the-tiger intensity that gave us the competitive advantage in the first place. On the other hand, there is playing "to focus and finish." Focus to *W-I-N* represents *W*hat's *I*mportant *N*ow. Then, we finish each play from "hello" to "goodbye," one play at a time, until we finish the game. Successful sales managers teach that anybody can make a presentation. It's closing the deal that wins the business. Successful parents teach, "If it's worth doing, it's worth doing right," and "If it's worth starting, it's worth finishing."

Whether it's halftime in your business year or in your life, whatever you do and wherever you are in life, don't let up now. Look beyond the halftime score. The only way you can win is to endure to the end!

Just a Little Extra Effort

Jim McMahon, the great quarterback for the 1985 Super Bowl Champion Chicago Bears, is the epitome of effort. From his days of Pop Warner football, through his high school, college and professional days, every time he walked on the field he knew he could win. Not by accident, fate, or fluke, but by extra effort.

It was December 19, 1980, Holiday Bowl III. Jim McMahon's nationally ranked Brigham Young University Cougars were playing against Southern Methodist University. There were four minutes and seven seconds left to play in the game. SMU was winning, 45–25. BYU called time-out, and Coach Lavell Edwards motioned McMahon to the sideline. Edwards said, "Let's see if we can save a little face and score before the game ends."

McMahon got upset. "Coach, what do you mean? We're not quitting! It's not over until it's over!" McMahon went back onto the field, called the team together, and said, "We're gonna win!" The very next play he threw a long pass—touchdown! BYU recovered the ensuing on-side kick and scored again on a one-yard scamper by a running back. BYU kicked off, held SMU for three downs, and then blocked the punt and recovered the ball with thirteen seconds left on the clock. McMahon's first two passes were incomplete, but on the very next play, with three seconds left in the game, McMahon completed a forty-six-yard bomb to Clay Brown in the end zone. Brown leaped high in the air to catch it and the game was tied! Gunther came onto the field and kicked the extra point. BYU won, 46–45.

In 1981, McMahon was runner-up to Marcus Allen for the Heisman Trophy, was the first-round pick by the Chicago Bears, and was named Rookie of the Year.

In 1984, Doug Flutie proved the same thing and, along with his Boston College teammates, won an important game in exactly the same miracle catch manner. Flutie also won the Heisman! These two athletes not only have superior talent, but they have the superior determination and drive that enables them to make the extra effort that always makes the difference. Not just in games, but more importantly, in practice.

The difference between good and great, between winning and losing, between receiving enormous rewards and no rewards at all, is just a little bit of extra effort.

> In 1974, the winning jockey of the Kentucky Derby received $27,000. The jockey who crossed the finish line in fourth place less than two seconds later received $30.
>
> In 1982, Gordon Johncock won the Indianapolis 500 by sixteen hundredths of a second, attributable to the length of his car. His paycheck was well over ten times that of the second place finisher, whom we don't even remember.
>
> In the 1984 Summer Olympic Games, the competitors in the women's long-distance cycling race engaged in a back-and-forth, hard-fought sprint to the finish line. The winner received the gold medal by the length of a bicycle wheel.
>
> In baseball, the difference between a .300 hitter who is a millionaire star and a .200 hitter who earns a minimal salary (and finds himself traded from team to team as often as a team manager changes his dirty socks) is one hit in every ten times at bat. And in those ten times at bat, if both these batters let their batting count go to "full-count" (three balls and two strikes), then the difference between them is only one hit in every sixty pitches!

Sure, it's important to have good practice facilities and great coaching—and also some talent to go with it. It's important to believe you are somebody special, equal to the guts and deserving of the glory of McMahon and Flutie. But without that little bit of extra effort, becoming a champion remains only a dream.

What Motivates Us?

There is a difference between inspiration and motivation. Inspiration affects our attitude—the way we think. Motivation affects our behavior—the way we act. For this reason, no one person can motivate another. All we can hope to do is inspire one another to each motivate ourselves. Motivation must come from within. Fear is a common motivator. Think of it as the do-it-or-else method. Reward is another common motivator, thought by many to be the best one of all. Yet, the only motivation that works all the time—regardless of the circumstances—is self-motivation. Self-motivation is self-discipline, which means "minding ourselves." Therefore, self-disciplined motivation means doing something simply because we want to do it and doing the right thing simply because it's the right thing to do—both are examples of lasting, top-notch motivation.

Motivation by fear may work temporarily, but only as long as the person instilling the fear in you is there. Motivation by reward doesn't work unless we choose the reward and, even then, the reward eventually loses its luster and charm—no external, material motivator can ever keep us motivated long-term. Enough is never enough.

Self-motivation, on the other hand, forces us to ask the question "Why should I?" The answer can only come from within. Arriving at the answer will help us discover what will satisfy our inner needs—whatever they may be.

Discover the joy of self-motivation—the joy of accomplishing an important goal because you wanted to, not because somebody forced you to do it by threatening dire consequences if you didn't, or coerced you to do it by promising you a reward if you did.

To stay focused, authentic, and motivated in all that you do, simply check and clean up your motives; be honest with yourself about why you do what you do, and replace any actions that are motivated externally with good, pure, powerful, positive self-motivation. Remember that it's what we do when the leader, manager, preacher, parent, coach, or teacher is not around that makes us champions!

Where Do Words Come From?

What we've been in the past does not make us who we are today. What we hope to become in the future does.

A few millennia ago, when written language was invented, a critic said, "The discovery of the alphabet will create forgetfulness in learners' souls because they will not use their memories. They will trust to the external written characters and not remember of themselves."

The critic's name was Socrates. Thanks to writing, we still remember much of what he said so long ago.

Centuries later, Gutenberg brought movable type and the printing press to the world. Critics said the same thing about print technology as they had about the invention of writing. A priest named Johannes Trithemius said printing would weaken the gift of memory so people would forget the vital words they memorized in church. Instead, printing has expanded our memories. Gutenberg's first printed book, the Bible, has been read and remembered more than any other book in history.

When television first arrived, critics said we would stop reading. In fact, television has stimulated reading. We have published, sold, and read more books since the invention of television than ever before. And we know more about what's happening throughout the world than ever before.

With the advent of the "information superhighway," we can gain instant access to all knowledge, everywhere in the world. Critics say the human mind can't handle it—the Worldwide Web is too much, and we'll lose our ability to remember and think.

Will the critics be wrong, once again?

As in the past, new information technologies will expand the human mind, improve learning skills, and make life better than it was yesterday.

The Art of Communication

Things aren't always what they seem to be. Perception isn't always reality. It should be, but it isn't. Too many people are outdoing by overdoing and, in the process, are eventually redoing reality.

When Emanuel Leutze painted *Washington Crossing the Delaware,* he depicted the Stars and Stripes being carried in the boat, even though the symbol was not adopted as the American flag until June 14, 1777—six months after Washington crossed the Delaware.

In his renowned oil painting, *Israelites Gather Manna in the Wilderness,* Tintoretto armed Moses' men with shotguns. The earliest known appearance of a gun was approximately AD 1326—somewhat after the Exodus!

In the biography *Abraham Lincoln: The Prairie Years,* Carl Sandburg wrote about Lincoln's mother singing "Greenland's Icy Mountain" as she stood at the family's log cabin door. Quite a feat, considering the song was not written until twenty-two years after Lincoln's death!

No wonder life seems so complicated. We bring it upon ourselves. Consider a bank, for instance: it's an institution where you can borrow money only if you present sufficient evidence that you don't need it.

What about the American voter who yells at the government to balance the budget and then borrows $50 "just until payday"? What about the father who cheats on his income taxes but can't understand why his son cheated on his math test? What about the mother who, while in the midst of lecturing her daughter about always being honest, hears the telephone ring and says, "Tell them I'm not here"?

It's true. Things aren't always what they should be. A firefly is actually a beetle—and if we have a bug called a fly why not a walk or a jog? A Douglas fir tree is actually a pine. A panda bear is actually a relative of the raccoon. An English horn is actually an alto oboe from France. A piece of catgut is actually made from sheep intestines. A Turkish bath is actually Roman.

The other day, even a reputable radio program threw me for a loop when the disc jockey said, "Now for a partial score—Chicago, 7." Those whom we expect will know what they are doing often don't. The United States Naval Academy of Design held an art competition and awarded second place to a work by Edward Dickenson. The judges later learned that the award-winning piece had been hanging upside down! At the signing of the Treaty of Versailles in 1919, David Lloyd-George of Great Britain advised the leader of Italy that his country could make up its commercial losses by increasing the production of its banana crop. This pronouncement neither heartened nor excited the man, since Italy does not produce bananas!

Today's world is even stranger: a woman pays $50 for a beautiful lace slip and gets annoyed if it shows beneath her dress; a man puts up screens to keep insects out of his home, air conditions his home, car, and office, then attends an outdoor picnic!

Let us stop the absurd madness of trying to be so sophisticated, complicated and grandiose. Simple, straightforward connection should be the required standard for all human interactions. It's the only way we will ever align our perception with reality. When we "tell it like it is," not only do we enjoy honest communication, but we also may find that our conversations are often entertaining!

When my son was five years old, his mother woke him up for the second day of kindergarten. He snapped, "What, again?"

When asked what hitting advice a batting instructor for the Seattle Mariners gives to player Ken Griffey, Jr., he replied, "I tell him, battaway, Junior!"

I heard two golden nuggets of straightforward, unadulterated truth the other day while I was at an airport. An elderly Southern woman was at the counter yelling at the top of her lungs, "Don't you lie to me. Don't you dare lie to me. If the pilot of this plane can fly in the dark and can find Springfield, Illinois, in a snowstorm, I know you can find my bag!" A man stood beside me with his suitcase on the floor next to him. The suitcase bore stickers from Hawaii, Toronto, Jamaica, Oklahoma, Utah, and Florida. Seeing the suitcase, the same woman blurted out, "My oh my, have you been to all those places?" The man replied, "No, but my luggage has!"

Quiet Heroes

The world is full of quiet heroes
Who never seek the praise.
They're always back off in the shadows
They let us have the lime-light days.
You're the one that I look up to
Because of you, I'm free
You set an example I could follow
You helped me see my destiny.

So even though my thanks don't show,
Unnoticed you will never go.
I need to say I love you so,
You're my hero!

I've had my share of broken dreams,
But you said I could win.
You gave me the chance I always needed
To start my dreams again.
You took the time to teach and tutor,
You showed me rules to rise.
You changed my fears to glory tears,
You're an angel in disguise.

So even though my thanks don't show,
Unnoticed you will never go.

I need to say I love you so,
You're my hero!

I wouldn't be where I am today,
I've won my share of time,
Unless you coached me through the maze
And pushed me on the hardest climbs.
It's just your style, the extra mile—
No glory must be tough.
You let me have the accolades,
A smile, you said, was just enough

So even though my thanks don't show,
Unnoticed you will never go.
I need to say I love you so,
You're my hero!

How Bad Do You Want It?

If you want a thing bad enough,
To go out and fight for it,
Work day and night for it,
Give up your time and your peace and your sleep for it,
If only the desire of it,
Makes you mad enough,
Never to tire of it,
Makes you hold all things tawdry and cheap for it,
If life seems all empty and useless without it,
And all that you scheme and dream is about it,
If you'll gladly sweat for it,
Fret for it,
Plan for it,
Lose all terror of God and man for it,
If you'll simply go after the thing that you want,
With all your capacity,
Strength and tenacity,
Faith, hope, and confidence, stern pertinacity,
If neither cold, poverty, famine, and haunt,
Nor sickness, nor pain
Of body or brain,
Can turn you away from the thing that you want,
If dogged and grim you besiege and beset it,
You'll get it.

Playing the Game

The best way to play any game in life is to give it your best shot. Many people miss out because they don't carry through to the end. So whenever you play a game or commit to a project, try to remember these words.

> Whatever the game, and whatever the odds,
> The winning is all up to you;
> For it isn't the score, and it isn't the prize
> That counts when the playing is through!
> In the great game of Life, it's the purpose to win
> And the courage to fight to the end
> That determines for you what degree of success
> Will be scored to your credit, my friend.
> The best you can do may not be quite enough
> To defeat your opponents today,
> But you never can lose, and you never can fail,
> If you put all you've got in your play.
> And the greatest reward that your efforts can bring
> Is the fact that you stood to the test—
> That you played a clean game and fought a good fight,
> And you always were doing your best!
> Anyone who gives their best, never really loses.

Perseverance

Two frogs fell into a bowl of cream.
One had an optimistic gleam,
But the other took the gloomy view.
"We'll drown," he cried, and without adieu
He gave a last despairing cry,
Flung up his legs, and said good-bye.
Said the other frog with a steady grin,
"I can't get out, but I won't give in;
I'll just swim around till my strength is spent,
Then will I die the more content."
Bravely he swam 'til it would seem
His struggles began to churn to cream.
On top of the butter at last he stopped,
And out of the bowl he gaily hopped.
What is the moral? It's easily found:
If you can't get out, keep swimming around.

Do As I Say

Leading by example is the only way to show that you mean what you say. This poem helps us understand the origin of morale. What is morale? It's the mental and emotional condition of a group of people as they face the tasks at hand. It includes confidence, enthusiasm, loyalty, and a common purpose.

No team wins if the team members are fighting among themselves.

How about rules? Do you respect the rules or break them? When rules are broken, even by one person, the team suffers.

Relaxing rules only causes morale to drop. We must be taught personal responsibility for our actions. Enthusiasm and purpose initiate morale, and rules sustain it. The great leaders in any organization make sure the people under them are following the rules. To do so requires that they lead by example. If you want to improve morale, it's not enough to practice what you preach. Preach only what you practice!

> I'd rather see a sermon preached than hear one any day.
> I'd rather someone walk with me than merely point the way.
> The eye's a better pupil and more willing than the ear.
> Fine counsel is confusing, but example is always clear.
> The finest preachers are the ones who live their creeds,
> To see good put into action is what everybody needs.
> I can learn to do it if you'll let me see it done.
> Your hand I see in action, your tongue too fast may run.
> And the lecture you deliver may be very well and true.

But I'd rather get my lesson by observing what you do.
For I might understand you, the high advice you give.
But there's no misunderstanding how you act and how you live.

Teaching Makes Other Professions Possible

There are people with college degrees and teaching certificates. There are people with teaching certificates who teach subjects. There are teachers who teach children. Then there are master teachers who teach children the practical application of the information.

Master teachers understand that the only place from which a person can grow is where he or she is. They must go where the student is physically and emotionally. Only there can they gently invite him or her to grow. Because of this belief in and dedication to the philosophy "whatever it takes," everything I need to know to be successful I learned from my master teachers. Somehow they always put "success" into their curriculum.

I remember my kindergarten master teacher, Mrs. Anderson. I can't tell you a lot about her or kindergarten; all I know is that I loved school. She made it fun and adventurous.

My first grade master teacher was Mrs. Dubois. She was as tough as her name sounds—doo bwau! She taught me that real love is based 100 percent on high expectations, discipline, and respect for authority. In retrospect, Mrs. Dubois' tough love—five days a week—was one of the best things that ever happened to me.

I don't remember second grade. I don't even remember my teacher's name. I guess it's because she only taught school instead of kids and life.

My third grade master teacher's name was Mrs. Inman. She obviously understood that the only place from which a person can grow is where he or she is. Every day, she sensitively and compassionately reached out to me, physically and emotionally, and gently invited me to grow.

To this day, I realize this one teaching technique is at the heart and soul of effective parenting, championship sales performance, and empowering administration. When I graduated from high school, I received a homemade card in the mail. On the inside left panel was a picture of a parakeet that I had drawn in the third grade. Under it was a poem I had written. It didn't rhyme at all. On the right side of the card was a newspaper clipping with me in my football uniform. Across the top of the card, printed in bold letters, were the simple words, "Congratulations. You've come a long way, baby. Love, Mrs. Sandy Inman, your third grade teacher."

My fourth grademaster teacher was Dr. Morray. Unbeknownst to anyone, Richard Wolfgram, the school bully, had been beating me up every single day. I went to school petrified and had to learn survival skills as I went. Dr. Morray never fought my battles but chose in her wisdom to clean up my face and hands, help me face my fears, grow in character and understanding, and develop mental toughness. To this day, I've never quit anything in my life, nor have I given up in any race, game, class, or situation, and I owe it all to Dr. Morray. I see counselors changing classes for students just because they don't like their teacher. I see parents protecting their children from the natural consequences of negative behavior. This is not good. In real life there are no counselors or protectors out there that allow us to run from our pain. A teacher's job is to prepare students for the real world so that when they get there, they will recognize it.

If everybody could have had a Dr. Morray in the fourth grade, our world would be so much stronger, self-reliant, and determined to endure to the end.

My fifth grade master teacher's name was Mrs. Dubois, again. She had changed grade levels in the nick of time!

My only memory of sixth grade, one which I try to forget, involved my two male teachers, Mr. A and Mr. G, who only caught me doing things wrong, didn't take the time to understand me, and labeled me a loser, which affected me for years.

In junior high school, I had three master teachers who touched my life forever. Mr. Millward taught band. I played the trumpet half the year and drums half the year in the seventh, eighth, and ninth grades. Mr. Millward stressed mastering the fundamentals. He taught that there are only twelve notes in music and that they were discovered way before Beethoven or B.B. King came along. What these masters did was take these twelve, basic notes and apply creativity and imagination to arrange them into magnificent, beautiful, musical masterpieces. Mr. Millward taught me to look not for new answers, but for the right answers. Because of Mr. Millward, I know that amidst our complex, changing world, there are still fundamental principles, natural laws and philosophies that remain constant, always true and unchanging.

The second junior high master teacher who put success into my curriculum was Mr. Penrod, who taught science. Going into the seventh grade, my friends and I thought Science would be boring. But Mr. Penrod was so passionate and excited about the subject that his enthusiasm became contagious. One day he got so carried away that he accidentally set himself on fire—we all thought that was pretty cool! Mr. Penrod didn't just write on a chalkboard, read from notes, and give homework assignments out of a textbook. Anybody can get a teaching certificate, but that doesn't make them educators. Mr. Penrod took the information off the board and out of the book and made it come alive. Ironically, it was Mr. Penrod, teaching a regimented, exact, formulated, equation-based science, who taught me that attitude is everything. Mr. Penrod helped me see that when your attitude is right, your ability will always catch up. "Sure," he used to say, "two plus two equals one specific sum regardless of whether you think positive or negative, but unless you have a positive, possibility-thinking attitude that you can and will discover the answer, you won't even attempt to solve the problem."

The third junior high master teacher that touched my life was Mr. Sorensen. He was a vocational technology educator who taught me wood shop the first half of the year and metal shop and electronics the second half. If you were to visit my home today, you would see a small oak stereo cabinet that slightly leans to the left and doesn't work very well. I built it in the seventh grade, and whenever I feel down, lose confidence, and don't comprehend that what I can do can have a lasting impact and be around for years to come, I simply look at that stereo cabinet and think to myself, "I followed directions and made a plan work and turn out like I thought it would. And what I've done once, I can surely do again.

To this day, I am the world's biggest fan of vocational education. Vocational education provides many student leadership organizations that all cater to the real needs of students by teaching hands on, practical application information in an understandable, usable way. Mr. Sorensen helped me see that teaching is just talking unless teachers and students truly connect. Explaining how and why and when to use each slice of our education is just as important as memorizing the facts. Thanks also to Coach Brooks, Coach Murry, Mr. Smith, Mr. Urry and Mrs. Richards, who taught me the fundamentals of diversity and team togetherness.

In high school, I had five master teachers who influenced my life forever. Mr. Croft epitomizes everything an educator needs to be. Amidst his education and curriculum preparation, he understood that example is still the best teacher. There are special stories about him included in this book, so for now let me say, I love and admire Mr. Croft. He is my hero!

The second master teacher was Coach Ted Weight, who was always there for me. He believed in me when no one else did. He didn't teach me just strategies, plays, and formations; he taught me to stay in bounds, play by the rules, get up each time I was knocked down, never say never, and never settle for anything less than my very best. I excelled in football, basketball, baseball, and track primarily because Coach Weight said I could if I worked hard. And he stuck by me while I did. I wouldn't have received any college scholarship offers or have succeeded in sports after high school if it hadn't been for Coach Weight.

Mr. Thoerum was the swimming coach who taught me college algebra and trigonometry. Going into the state basketball tournament, our team was ranked number one in the state. Tournament officials checked each player's academic records for eligibility, and they determined that I was failing trigonometry, which meant that my entire team was ineligible. My coach commanded me to do something about it.

I approached Mr. Thoerum to see what I could do to pass. He explained that his all-state swimmer had been ineligible to compete in their state meet and that his teacher had not cut him any slack. He failed him, and the young man did not swim in the meet. He would have broken records and helped his team to victory, but the team lost without him. Mr. Thoerum's question to me was why should he do me a favor? Why should I receive special treatment? My only comeback was that at least the rest of the swimming team could compete, even if the ineligible kid didn't. If I failed his class the whole basketball team was out of luck. He gave me a tough take-home test to complete over the weekend and made me a deal. If I got all the problems correct and could explain in detail exactly how I arrived at the answers, I would pass his class. It was a comprehensive test that covered the entire semester. I knew he didn't think I could do it. That weekend, I worked with tutors, my nuclear physicist uncle, and my dad, and I passed the test and that class. For the rest of my life, I will love and admire Tom Thoerum, who taught me to pull for the underdog and give the deserving a break.

The fourth high school teacher who touched my life forever was Mr. "Lefty" Bennett. He taught AP History and Constitutional Law in a way that was passionate, memorable, and exceptionally relevant. He always supported my athletic games as a visible spectator, so I was more inclined to work hard in his class and not let him down. His son, Mike, is now a superintendent who holds the same ideals of excellence—a chip off the old block!

The last of five high school educators who put success into my curriculum was Mrs. Smart, my AP English teacher. She instilled in me a love of words, a desire to read and to be a life-long learner, and a yearning to express myself as a writer. Teaching truly is the profession that makes all other professions possible!

0 26575 70411 2